COVEY

A Stone's Throw from a Coal Mine to the Hall of Fame

The life story of Stan Coveleski,
who escaped the Pennsylvania coal mines and
became a Hall-of-Fame baseball pitcher.

Harry J. Deitz Jr.

SUNBURY
PRESS ®

Mechanicsburg, PA USA

Published by Sunbury Press, Inc.
Mechanicsburg, PA USA

SUNBURY
P R E S S ®

www.sunburypress.com

For information about special discounts for bulk purchases, please contact Sunbury Press
Orders Dept. at (855) 338-8359 or orders@sunburypress.com.

To request one of our authors for speaking engagements or book signings, please contact
Sunbury Press Publicity Dept. at publicity@sunburypress.com.

FIRST SUNBURY PRESS EDITION: July 2022

Set in Adobe Garamond Pro | Interior design by Crystal Devine | Cover by Lawrence Knorr | Edited by
Lawrence Knorr.

Publisher's Cataloging-in-Publication Data
Names: Deitz Jr., Harry J., author.
Title: Covey : a stone's throw from a coal mine to the Hall of Fame / Harry J. Deitz Jr.
Description: First trade paperback edition. | Mechanicsburg, PA : Sunbury Press, 2022.
Summary : Stanley Coveleski's life was a story of triumph and tragedy. He escaped the Pennsylvania coal
mines by throwing stones at tin cans—his way of learning how to pitch a baseball. By 1920, a season
marked by the death of his wife and his teammate Ray Chapman, he won three games in the World Series
and went on to become a Hall of Fame pitcher.
Identifiers: ISBN : 978-1-62006-081-0 (softcover).
Subjects: BIOGRAPHY & AUTOBIOGRAPHY / Sports | SPORTS & RECREATION / Baseball /
History | SPORTS & RECREATION / Baseball / General.

Product of the United States of America
0 1 1 2 3 5 8 13 21 34 55

Continue the Enlightenment!

Cover photo: Stan Coveleski during his playing days with the Cleveland Indians. (Photo is from the
Ernie Harwell Sports Collection, Detroit Public Library, and used with permission.)

To my father, Harry J. Deitz,
another Shamokin legend,
who introduced me to journalism and writing.

Contents

Foreword

Who was the greatest baseball pitcher born in Pennsylvania? It would make for an interesting debate. Most would argue Factoryville's Christy Mathewson should take the prize. Residents from Adam's County would push Eddie Plank to the front or argue he was the best lefthander and Mathewson the best righthander. After these two, the rest of the crowd have remained relatively anonymous since their retirements, despite making the Hall of Fame. A great trivia question would be: Name all the Hall of Fame pitchers born in Pennsylvania. Do you know the remaining six?

No, you can't pick Chief Bender. While he was raised at the Carlisle Indian School and went on to greatness, he was born in Minnesota. Likewise, Pud Galvin, who is buried in Pittsburgh but was born in St. Louis.

Montoursville's Mike Mussina would come to mind for many people, given his recent induction and connection to the New York Yankees. That's one of six.

Lancaster's Bruce Sutter would come to mind for many older fans who remember his diving split-finger fastball from the 1970s and 1980s. That's two of six.

Rube Waddell was born in Bradford, Pennsylvania, and lived a short life full of excitement and self-inflicted trouble. That's three of six.

Ed Walsh, born in Plains, Pennsylvania, won 40 games in one season but finished with fewer than 200 wins due to injuries. That's four of six.

A couple of years ago, while researching our Keystone Tombstones series, Joe Farrell, Joe Farley, and I were at Union Hill Cemetery in Kennett Square, Pennsylvania, to visit the grave of the lovely late actress Linda Darnell. When asking for directions to her grave, the groundskeeper said,

"And you know we have a Hall-of-Fame pitcher, too." At that point, I was shocked my prior research did not remind me of Herb Pennock, the Yankee lefthander. Now we're at five of six.

The last gentleman on the list is a native of Shamokin, Pennsylvania, but is buried in Indiana. He won 215 games in his career and had five 20-win seasons. He was a hero of the 1920 Cleveland world champions, winning three games in that World Series. Stan Coveleski completes the list of six.

Oddly, until now, no one has tackled writing a biography about "Covey." He transitioned from the Deadball Era to the Live-Ball Era without sacrificing much. This is likely due to being one of the grand-fathered spitballers who were permitted to keep throwing the pitch for the remainder of their careers. My previous exposure to him was while reading Lawrence Ritter's classic *The Glory of Their Times*, perhaps the best baseball history ever written. Ritter dedicated a chapter to Covey. He was one of the veterans still alive when Ritter did his research, unlike Eddie Plank, who had passed in 1926. Eugene Murdock also interviewed Coveleski in his oral history. These are probably the longest treatments of Coveleski's career besides his biography at SABR.

Now Harry Deitz has tackled this long-overdue task. Harry was motivated by highlighting a fellow Shamokin citizen, the town's only Hall-of-Fame player. We can't say "only major leaguer" because brother Harry Coveleski was a star pitcher until he was injured and Jake Daubert, the line-drive machine at first base, are also from Shamokin. Nevertheless, Harry Deitz brings us new material from interviews and local sources. Once again, we can relive those early years of major league baseball while Babe Ruth and Ty Cobb were still taking the field. Enjoy!

Lawrence Knorr
Author of *Gettysburg Eddie: The Story of Eddie Plank*
June 2022

Preface

Stanislaus Anthony Kowalewski was born in 1889 in the Coal Region town of Shamokin, Pennsylvania. Sixty-three years later, I drew my first breath in that same community. That's where our similarities end, but it was enough to spark my interest in learning about the life and preserving the memory of a man who became one of the town's greatest legends.

It's a story about a young boy who escaped a dangerous and uninspiring life as a coal miner to become a Hall of Fame baseball pitcher.

It's also a story of a man whose accomplishments are remembered less in his hometown with each passing generation.

Stan Coveleski, as he was known during his baseball career, was the youngest of five sons of Polish immigrants who settled in the mining patch of Fidler's Green, which he called "the Fidler." He was uneducated, but he had a strong drive to succeed. Whenever he found a few hours of daylight from his work in the mines, he threw stones at a can tied to a tree. Was it just to pass the time, or did he have a secret plan that the repetition would lead to a better life by following his brothers out of the mines and onto the baseball fields?

He probably didn't talk much about his dreams then. In fact, he was a quiet person, shy and soft-spoken throughout his life, and eventually acquired the nickname the "Silent Pole." Whatever lack of confidence he may have had in life disappeared when he stepped onto a pitcher's mound several years later.

Covey (KO-vee), as he referred to himself, had become so good at hitting that can with rocks he collected that he retained the same control when he picked up a baseball as a teenager and fired it into the mitt of a catcher.

That perfected repetition and his development a few years later of a legal spitball put him on a path to become one of the greatest pitchers of the 1920s, which eventually was rewarded with his election to the National Baseball Hall of Fame in 1969.

There are numerous statistics and accounts from his professional baseball career. He won 215 games during 14 seasons, won three games to lead the Cleveland Indians to the 1920 World Series championship, and played with and pitched against some of the greatest men in the history of baseball, including Babe Ruth, Ty Cobb, Tris Speaker, Shoeless Joe Jackson, and Walter "Big Train" Johnson. He pitched on the day teammate Ray Chapman was hurt and became the only player in baseball history to die from being hit by a pitched ball. He was a teammate of Ray Caldwell, who was struck by lightning, then got up and finished the game.

All of those are interesting stories, but what about the man? What about his life before and after baseball? And what about his family?

During my research for this book, I reached out to people to learn as much as possible about Stan's life in Shamokin before his baseball career and about his life in South Bend after his career. But many people who knew him are gone, and the stories about his life off the baseball field are scarce.

In South Bend, a minor league stadium was named in his memory, even though the naming rights for the field later were sold to a casino. As a tradeoff, team owners erected a life-size statue of him at that stadium.

In Shamokin, community leaders were sparked by long-time local radio personality Tom Kutza to memorialize Covey and his Hall-of-Fame induction with a monument made to look like a large chunk of coal. It was dedicated in 1997. Even so, not everyone knows about one of the greatest players ever to come out of the coal region. In my search for information, one young person I spoke with didn't know who he was or that there was a physical tribute to him on Market Street.

That's why this book is important. It's not only to recognize his career, but it's also a history book written to make sure the Silent Pole is not forgotten.

Many years ago, when I first considered writing this book, I didn't know much more about him than that he was in the Hall of Fame and was born and raised in Shamokin. During my research, I discovered one interesting story after another about the difficulties and tragedies he overcame and the success he enjoyed. Whenever I learned something about his life, I wanted to know more about him.

I learned that he was quiet and shy, but his confidence surged when he stepped onto a pitcher's mound. He hated to lose and wanted to be left alone when he didn't. He had a lifelong interest in hunting, and his offseason walks in the woods helped him stay in shape for baseball. Fishing became another passion during his playing days and in retirement. Even though he lacked formal education, he was very knowledgeable about baseball and, even in his later years, could remember how to pitch to the best hitters during his career.

From the time he started working at the colliery at age 12 until he died at 94, he chewed tobacco. He was among the last of the great spitball pitchers in the 1920s, but he had excellent control and was a good pitcher before he learned to throw the spitter.

I sense that he was very proud of his baseball career, but not to the point of arrogance or self-importance. When he spoke about his accomplishments, it was honestly and matter-of-fact. What he didn't seem to share much was the pain of several personal tragedies in his life.

Numerous times I found myself wishing I could have met him. I am thankful to those who did—Tom Kutza, Rod Roberts, Eugene Murdock, and Lawrence S. Ritter, who conducted audio interviews with Covey many years after his baseball career. Their conversations helped me learn a little about the man and how he remembered his childhood and playing days. I appreciate the family members who shared memories of their Uncle Stan from their childhoods, especially Rosalie Coveleski Moyer, who talked about her experiences and put me in contact with other descendants. A special thank-you to Bruce Victoriano, his father Ralph, and genealogist Dr. Ann Yezerski, who helped me track down information about Stan's family. And I am grateful for the advice and direction from baseball historians and authors Scott Longert and Steve Steinberg.

It was a challenge when looking back at a career from 100 years ago when there was no television to provide visual history. Family members struggled to share memories because many of them were young during his later years. Finding non-baseball records was difficult, not just because record-keeping was sketchy 120 years ago, but also because of the variations of his family name, including the original Kowalewski, pronounced ko-va-LESS-kee, but which often was written Kovalewski, Koveleski, Covaleski, Coveleskie, and his preferred Coveleski. During his playing days, most newspapers used the spelling Coveleskie, but the final word was on his tombstone—Coveleski—which I have used in this book, except when quoted in printed articles.

The various spellings are another thing to which I can relate because most people have trouble remembering my name is spelled Deitz, not Dietz.

Now, if only I could have shared his ability to throw a baseball over a plate, or at least throw a stone and hit a tin can . . .

1

From darkness into darkness

In the early morning hours, before the sun rose above the hills that rim the town, a group of coal miners walked quietly and steadily along a dirt road toward the deep hole that would be their home for the next 12 hours. There, in darkness that the sunlight couldn't erase, they worked stooped over or lying on their backs or bellies, chipping away at the Anthracite coal cemented deep beneath their community. Darkness was a way of life for these miners.

The hammering and digging hardened their arms and hands, and the sharp rocks of coal and slate scarred their skin. They always carried with them some of the dirt of the previous day that was embedded under their fingernails and tattooed onto their flesh despite rigorous scrubbing every night. The dust from their labor filled the air and settled deep into their lungs.

They feared for cave-ins or gas that could spark explosions but not enough to abandon the means of support for their families. If those threats didn't cut short their lives, black-lung disease from the coal dust eventually might. Or perhaps they would become a victim of some form of cancer from the tobacco they chewed continuously to battle the dirt in the air.

If they were lucky enough to survive the working conditions, they earned a wage that barely supported their families. There was little hope and few opportunities to find a better life in the Anthracite coal region at the end of the nineteenth century.

In 1901, at 12 years of age, Stanislaus Anthony Kowalewski left his house in the Fidler's Green patch southeast of Shamokin and joined that fraternity of miners. For 11 or 12 hours a day, six days a week, he and 40 or 50 other young boys would pick slate from the coal the men and older boys brought out of the mine that ran deep under the communities of Shamokin and Coal Township. Stan's rewards were $3.75 per week – about five cents an hour – and rough and bloodied hands from handling the sharp chunks of coal and slate.

After one year, he quit school, which provided little promise for his future. He often wondered if this was all life was about. It was the world his Polish-immigrant father and his four older brothers knew. After 12 grueling hours, there was a sense of relief each evening as they survived another day and escaped the darkness of the mine to walk home in the darkness of the night. That future seemed to be set for young Stan and his brothers.

Despite that eventual reality, many of the miners had come to the United States from Europe in hopes of building a better life for their families.

"When the new generation of steamships came about, there were literally in Europe hundreds of agents of American companies that were trying to recruit people to come and work in the coal mines," explained Steve Steinberg, a historian who has written numerous books about the early years of baseball. "And as hard as it is to believe, for these people, it was a wonderful improvement in their lives. The steamship companies were basically subsidized by the coal companies, and you could come to America for free. Typically, you came and settled in somewhere, and then you sent for your wife and children at a later time."[1]

The Anthracite coal fields were in Sullivan, Lackawanna, Luzerne, Carbon, Schuylkill, Dauphin, Northumberland, and Columbia counties in the northeastern part of Pennsylvania, according to a 1916 report by the Department of the Interior, Bureau of Mines.[2]

"Coal, or 'Black Diamonds,' was first discovered around 1870 in what later would become Kulpmont, where Isaac Tomlinson picked some pieces out of Quaker Run and took them into Berks County for a blacksmith to try," according to the City of Shamokin website, shamokincity.org: "Mr. Tomlinson erected a blacksmith shop and used Shamokin Stone Coal. From this small beginning emerged an industrial giant, 'coal,' which was to play a big part of the Industrial Revolution and played an even more revolutionary role in the development of the city.

"The town of Shamokin was laid out on March 1, 1835. Later, the tract of land known as Groveville just to the west of the town was added. The town was formed in the true tradition of a Melting Pot with English, Welsh, Irish, Italian, Polish, Lithuanian, and German immigrants. Places of worship sprouted to serve the masses: Roman Catholic, Methodist, Presbyterian, Baptist, Lutheran, and Jewish. The city grew beyond mining to include bakeries, ice cream, and dairy factories, F&S Brewery, Eagle Silk Mill, dress and hosiery factories, as well as three movie theaters. The Borough of Shamokin was incorporated in 1864. Several other names were suggested for the name of the borough—Boyd's Quarry, Boydtown, Newtown, and Marion. John Boyd named the borough Shamokin."

The name Shamokin came from the language of the Delaware Indians and means "Eel Creek." Thomas Alva Edison established the Edison Illuminating Company of Shamokin in 1882, and St. Edward's is said to have been the first church in the world to have electricity. By 1920, the Eagle Silk Mill became what was believed to be the largest textile building under one roof in the United States. And the large mountain of discarded culm—the dirt washed and screened from the coal—that rose along the northern boundary of Shamokin was proudly referred to as the largest manmade mountain in the world. By 1920 the population of Shamokin and Coal Township was about 50,000.

All of that grew out of the discovery of coal.

People had come by the thousands from European countries seeking opportunities. Among them was Anthony Kowalewski, Stan's father, born in Poland in 1846. In 1870, he married Antonina Racicz, who was born in 1850, also in Poland. The couple boarded a ship to New York in 1873, then made their way to the growing mining community of Shamokin, located in the lower part of the Anthracite coal fields in northeastern Pennsylvania, where there was plenty of work.

Anthony and Antonina, sometimes called Antonette or Anna, settled in a small patch called Fidler's Green, about a mile southeast of Shamokin and near Springfield, Coal Run, and Luke Fidler in the adjacent Coal Township. Like many other families, they lived in housing they rented from the mining company, learned to speak English, raised their children, and attended the local Catholic church every Sunday. About 1875, their first son Jacob was born, followed by Sophia in 1879, Francis (Frank) in 1881, Margaret in 1882, John in 1884, Harry in 1886, Stan in 1889, and Helen in 1890. All five boys would become good baseball players, but first, they became miners. As soon as each boy was old enough, he quit school and joined his father in the mines.

The men worked long hours for pay that didn't nearly compensate for the dangerous conditions. The story of those early years of mining was that mine owners often became very wealthy while their workers struggled to pay rent and feed their families and prayed to stay alive.

"During the period 1870 to 1913, inclusive, 17,716 fatalities occurred in and about the anthracite mines, representing a rate of 3.42 per 1,000 men employed. The amount of coal mined per fatality was 124,968 tons, or there were eight fatalities per million tons mined," according to a Department of the Interior, Bureau of Mines report, "Coal-mine fatalities in the United States 1870-1914."[3]

In the mid- to late-1800s, violence escalated, and strikes took place throughout the region because of low wages, dangerous conditions, and discrimination. After mine owners broke the Workingmen's Benevolent Association union's "Long Strike of 1875," the infamous Molly Maguires supposedly emerged in the Anthracite coal region. According to the Pennsylvania Historical & Museum Commission, the Molly Maguires may have "originated in Ireland in the 1840s as a secret society dedicated to fighting the mounting agricultural oppressions in their country."[4]

Men who were believed to be associated with the Molly Maguires were charged with numerous murders of mining officials, and on June 21, 1877, 10 of the 20 who were accused and sentenced to death were hanged on what was called Black Thursday.

The poor conditions also led to the establishment of the Department of Mines on April 14, 1903,[5] to monitor safety and report accidents, but mining remained a dangerous profession.

Stan had heard the stories of fatal mine accidents and explosions, including where they worked at the Luke Fidler Colliery, along present-day Route 61, where a McDonald's restaurant is now located. In 1894 a miner had carried an open lamp into the mine and set off a fire that killed five men. The mine had to be flooded to extinguish the fire, which caused the shutdown of that mine and the connected Hickory Ridge Colliery and put approximately 1,000 men out of work for months. In 1902 another explosion claimed the lives of seven men at the Luke Fidler mine.[6]

With low pay, long days, dangerous conditions, and serious health threats, Stan understood that the best outcome of working in the mines would be living to tell about it.

After working as a breaker boy for a few years, he became a mule-team driver, hauling timbers into the mine to frame the tunnels where the men would enter and return with carloads of black rocks. That provided a little more money while limiting his exposure to the dangers deep in the mines, but his future remained bleak.

American baseball was in its infancy at the time. It didn't yet exist as a goal that young men with strength and athletic ability could aspire to reach and provide a life far better than what they could achieve in the coal mines, although that began to change in the early 1900s. For the young Kowalewski boys and their friends, baseball became recreation in their rare free time and, if they were lucky, a possible way to earn a little extra money.

Stan's primary release from his bleak future and the danger he faced daily was from throwing stones at a tin can. In the summer evenings, when there still was some daylight after his mine shift and on Sundays, he would tie a can to a tree or set it on a log, step back 40 or 50 feet and throw stone after stone at the can. He became very good at hitting the can, but at that time, he didn't imagine it would be his ticket out of the coal mines.

The Luke Fidler Colliery around 1915. (Photo courtesy of Larry Deklinski.)

Breaker boys sorting coal in an Anthracite coal breaker in 1911. (Photograph by Lewis Hine for the National Child Labor Committee collection. Courtesy of the Library of Congress.)

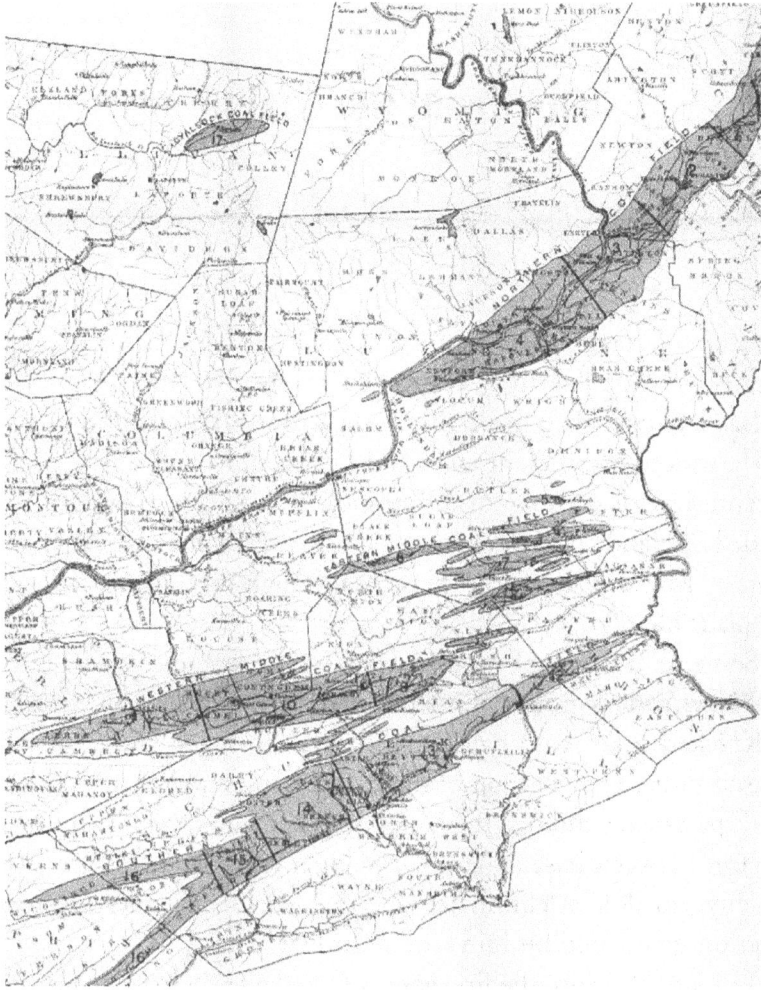

Map showing the Anthracite Coalfields of Pennsylvania. Luke Fidler and Shamokin are located in the western part of the Middle Fields. (Courtesy of Pennsylvania State University Libraries.)

2

Escape from the coal mines

By the start of the twentieth century, baseball had become America's game. Contrary to a popular myth, it was not invented by Abner Doubleday.

"Baseball likely had its origins in the early 1800s, possibly as a mash-up of a variety of different stick-and-ball games that had been around for centuries," according to Britannica. "These proto-baseball games included England's cricket or rounders and even games played in ancient Egypt, by Mayan tribes, or in France, although the England story is the most plausible.

"Some semblances of what baseball would become can be traced to 1800s New York as groups of men started crafting their own sets of rules. The Knickerbocker Base Ball Club of New York gets the credit for the first true effort, with a group of men on the rules committee outlining a 20-rule parameter, dubbed the Knickerbocker Rules, which set foul lines, the paces between bases, the limit of three outs, and, (in a safety-first mentality, no doubt) eliminated the dodgeball-style rule that to get a runner out you could hit him with a thrown ball."[1]

On June 19, 1846, the first game of baseball as it became known was played in New Jersey when the New York Mutuals defeated the Knickerbockers, 23-1.[2] In 1876 the National League of Professional Baseball Clubs was formed and became known as the National League. The American League was organized in 1901. The first World Series between the leagues was held in 1903.

In the coal fields of Pennsylvania, baseball was a welcomed diversion from the harsh reality of working long days in dangerous coal mines.

On Sundays, the only day the mines were closed, and on summer evenings when there was enough daylight after the miners' 12-hour shifts, the young men and boys would get together, choose up sides and play baseball.

Stan's four older brothers were among those baseball players. Eventually, he would join them, just as he had joined them in the mines. Meanwhile, he was refining his skill by spending most of his free time throwing stones at tin cans.

In 1907 Stan's brother Harry left Shamokin and the mines to pitch for Kane, Pennsylvania, in the Inter-State League, which disbanded during the season.[3] He had a brief callup by the Philadelphia Phillies in the fall of that year but in 1908 was optioned to the Lancaster Red Roses team in the Tri-State League.

One day in the fall of 1908, Stan was throwing stones near his home when Charlie Lewis, a teacher at the Springfield school, watched him and asked him if he'd like to pitch for Shamokin in the Atlantic League.[4] He agreed, and that fall played in his first organized games. Many years later, Stan recalled pitching in five games at the field at Springfield and winning all five that fall, although some records show him with a 6-2 record.

"When I pitched in those five ballgames, it came out in the Lancaster paper," Stan recalled during his 1969 interview with Tom Kutza. "Harry was with Lancaster at that time, and they asked Harry who this Coveleski was. He said, 'I don't know.' They asked if he has a brother. He said, 'Yes, but he don't play ball.' But I did play ball.

"That fall, me and Frank Lewis and John (Stan's brother) were in to see a show, and they come out on the stage and asked if Stanley Coveleski was there. They said he's wanted at the box office. I said, 'John, something must have happened at home.' So, we go down there, and (Lancaster Red Roses manager) Marty Hogan's down there, and he said, 'I want to sign you to a contract.' So, he took me to the (Graemar) hotel. So up to this time, I'm driving four mules and a skid and getting $9 a week. He put a contract to me for $250, and I didn't have enough nerve to sign it. So, he finally signed John up and he signed Frank Lewis up, and finally, I signed up."[5]

Baseball took Stan out of Shamokin, but more importantly, it gave him a path out of the coal mines. He and his brothers earned more money playing baseball than they had in the mines, and they sent it home to their mother to help support the family.

Stan and John joined a team that included future major leaguers Roxey Roach, John Wesley "Snake" Deal, and Ed Fitzpatrick. The Red Roses won the Tri-State League championship in 1909 with a 75-39 record. Stan, a right-handed pitcher who threw a fastball, curveball, and knuckleball at the time, had a 23-11 record and a 1.95 ERA in 272 innings.[6] His brother John played the outfield and some at third base and batted .291 with four home runs in 413 plate appearances. Harry had left Lancaster before the end of the 1908 season to join the Philadelphia Phillies.

Stan played for the Red Roses for two more years, going 15-8 with a 2.01 ERA in 1910 and 15-19 and 2.81 in 1911. In 1912 he played for the Lancaster (Ohio) Lanks team, which relocated to Atlantic City in June, and was 20-14 with a 2.53 ERA.

Covey wasn't the only Shamokin native to escape the coal mines through baseball. All of Stan's brothers were good baseball players. The most successful of them was Harry, three years older than Stan and a left-handed pitcher.

When the Philadelphia Phillies called up Harry in September of 1908, he pitched and won three games in five days against the New York Giants, denying them of the National League pennant and earning him the fabled nickname "Giant Killer." He had an 81-55 record during nine years with the Phillies, Cincinnati Reds, and Detroit Tigers, including winning 22, 22, and 21 games from 1914-1916 with the Tigers. Harry's major-league career was winding down as Stan's was taking off, ending his career in 1918. He returned to Shamokin, where he worked as a police officer for four years before opening a bar, The Giant Killer Café, at 602 North Liberty Street.

John played in the minor leagues between 1908 and 1917 for Shamokin, Wilmington Peaches, Lancaster Red Roses, San Antonio Bronchos, Albany Senators, Atlantic City, Reading Pretzels, Erie Sailors, Muskegon Reds, and Richmond Quakers. In 909 games, he had a .272 batting average and 12 home runs. He had a couple of tryouts, including with Connie Mack's Philadelphia Athletics, but never made a major-league roster.

Jacob, born 14 years before Stan and the oldest of the brothers, worked in the mines and played baseball as a pitcher before he was killed while serving in the Spanish-American War in 1898. The cause was drowning, and his body was lost at sea. Frank also pitched, but his career ended because of rheumatism before reaching the majors.

John, Harry, and Stan were listed as ballplayers in the 1910 census.

Several other Shamokin natives also left the mines to play in the majors, the most notable of which was Jacob Ellsworth Daubert. Gentleman Jake was born on April 7, 1884. During his 15-year major-league career, the left-handed first-baseman played for the Brooklyn Superbas (1910–1913), the Brooklyn Robins (1914–1918), and the Cincinnati Reds (1919–1924). He had a career batting average of .303 with 56 home runs and 165 triples in 2,014 games and won batting titles in 1913 (.350) and 1914 (.329) during baseball's Deadball Era. He was an excellent first-baseman, leading the National League three times in fielding percentage.

Daubert captained the World Series champion Reds in 1919 when they defeated the Chicago White Sox in a series that was better known for the Black Sox scandal when eight Chicago players were later banned from the game for life for taking money from gamblers to throw the series. Daubert played for the Robins in 1916 when they lost the World Series to the Boston Red Sox.

He died on October 9, 1924, in Cincinnati, about a month after his last game, and is buried in Charles Baber Cemetery, Pottsville, Pennsylvania. Earlier that year, he was beaned—one of eight beanings during his career—and suffered from headaches and sleeplessness for the rest of the season. After experiencing abdominal pain at the end of the season, he was operated on for suspected appendicitis and gallstones but died a week later. The cause of death eventually was attributed to a hereditary condition related to his spleen.[7]

Harry Budson Weiser, known as Bud Weiser, was born on January 8, 1891. He had one of the great baseball names but only had 74 at-bats in 41 games, batting .161 during the 1915 and 1916 seasons as an outfielder with the Philadelphia Phillies. Weiser did not play for the Phillies in the 1915 World Series, when they lost to the Boston Red Sox, 4-1. He died on July 31, 1961, in Shamokin and is buried in the Odd Fellows Cemetery.[8]

George Lewis Gilham was born on September 17, 1899. He played in one game in each of the 1920 and 1921 seasons as a catcher with the St. Louis Cardinals and was hitless in four at-bats. He died on April 25, 1937, in Lansdown, Pennsylvania, and is buried in the Shamokin Cemetery.[9]

The 1909 Lancaster Red Roses. Stan Coveleski is fourth from the left in the back row. (Photo is in the public domain and was obtained from Wikimedia Commons.)

Stan Coveleski

Jake Kowalewski

John Coveleskie

Frank Coveleskie

Harry Coveleski

Photos from the program for the Shamokin testimonial to honor Stan Coveleski in 1969, courtesy of Bruce Victoriano and Tom Kutza.

3

A miner in the minors

Stan Coveleski was quiet and shy from the time he was a boy. That, no doubt, was why he refused to sign with the Lancaster team in 1908 when he was 19 until Red Roses Manager Marty Hogan also signed Stan's older brother John.

"You know, I was never out of Shamokin before," he told Tom Kutza in 1969. "I was never on a train in my life. When I went to Lancaster, eating in the hotel, I was so bashful I used to sneak away and eat hot dogs on the side street."[1]

He recalled that some of his teammates wondered why they didn't see him in the hotel dining room, so one day, they followed him. After that, they made him join them for meals.

He retained those reserved traits throughout his life. As a boy, when he wasn't working or throwing stones at cans, young Covey would take his bird dogs and head into the mountains alone to hunt. In his August 22, 1981, recorded audio interview with Rod Roberts, Stan recalled himself as "the most bashful kid that ever lived" and said if a girl looked at him, he'd just turn his head. He said all his brothers were quiet, and "if you want a word, you gotta coax it out of them. You keep out of trouble."[2]

Stan was much more confident when he stepped onto the pitcher's mound. He often talked about the importance of control and said he could throw the baseball wherever the catcher placed his mitt. He attributed that to being able to throw a stone and hit a can, which he believed was harder than throwing a baseball over a 17-inch-wide home plate.

In the four seasons after he left the mines and played in the minors with Lancaster and Atlantic City, Stan was 73-52 with a 2.35 ERA in 1,070 innings. His success with Lancaster caught the attention of Connie Mack, the manager and owner of the American League Philadelphia Athletics, who called him up to the majors in the fall of 1912.

Covey made his major-league debut at age 23 on September 10, 1912, in Detroit against the Tigers at Navin Field. He pitched the eighth inning, faced four batters, didn't allow a hit or a run, and walked one. The Athletics lost to the Tigers, 8-6.[3]

The next day against the Tigers, he walked the only batter he faced in the ninth inning of the Athletics' 9-7 victory.

On September 12, pitching for the third straight day, he started against Detroit and pitched a complete-game, three-hit shutout, which the A's won, 3-0. Covey didn't know anything about the batters, so catcher Ben Egan told him to just throw to his glove. He struck out three and walked one. A double by Ty Cobb and singles by Bobby Veach and Eddie Onslow were the only hits for Detroit. The game was played in one hour and forty minutes before 4,002 fans.

The next day *The Philadelphia Inquirer* reported: "Never did he permit two Tigers to stray to first base in one inning. Ty Cobb was the only man to get further than the first corner, he pulling off one of his specialties of stretching a single into a double. Pops, both foul and fair, weak grounders and a few hoists to the garden constituted the extent of the Bengal efforts with the war club."[4]

On September 18, he lost the first game of a doubleheader to the Chicago White Sox, 9-1, pitching a complete game, allowing 14 hits, striking out three, and walking one. He got his first hit in that game.

His final appearance with the A's was on September 30 at Shibe Park, when he got the win against the New York Highlanders in relief of Athletics starter Bullet Joe Bush, who gave up 10 runs and 15 hits in eight innings. Covey pitched the final three innings, striking out three, allowing no runs or walks and only one hit. Philadelphia scored in the bottom of the 11th to win, 11-10.

In five games with Philadelphia, he was 2-1 with a 3.43 ERA. In 21 innings, he struck out nine, walked four, and hit one batter. The A's finished third in the American League in 1912 with a 90-61-1 record, but the team was a powerhouse in the first half of that decade. Philadelphia won World Series championships in 1910, 1911, and 1913 and lost in the 1914 Series after winning its fourth American League title in five seasons.

Covey's first experience in the majors showed promise, and he respected Connie Mack and how he treated players. He said when a player made a mistake, Mack wouldn't "bawl anybody out" on the bench but would ask the player to take a walk with him after the game.[5]

Those five games, however, were the only ones he would play for the legendary manager because the A's had a loaded pitching staff, including Charles Chief Bender, Jack Coombs, Eddie Plank, Boardwalk Brown, Joe Bush, and Byron Houck, leaving no room for the young Coveleski at the start of the 1913 season. So, Mack sent him to gain some experience in the minors with the Spokane Indians, with whom Mack had a working agreement, in the B-level Northwestern League.

After four years of playing baseball, Stan's move across the country was less traumatic than when he had left Shamokin. He was 17-20 in his first year in Spokane, then improved to 20-15 in 1914. That earned him a promotion to Class AA Pacific Coast League Portland, which had a working agreement with the Cleveland Indians. Reportedly when Mack inquired why Covey was sent to Portland, he was told the Athletics' rights to Coveleski had expired. In Portland, he learned a skill that would change his career.

The confidence that Stan had on the mound must have helped him in his life off the baseball field, including with girls, because on February 11, 1915, he married Mary Shivetts from his hometown Shamokin in St. Stanislaus Church. Like Stan, her family had come from Poland, and her father worked in the Shamokin coal mines. A short time later, they traveled to Portland, where they lived at 781 Kearney Street.

Although he was advancing, Covey began to wonder if he was on a path back to the majors. At the start of the 1915 season, he was 25 and in his seventh year in the minors. He had good control of his fastball, slowball, and curve, but he believed he needed something more.

When he joined Portland, he watched one of the pitchers throwing a spitball and decided he would start working on that pitch. He had chewed tobacco since he was 12, so he wet his fingers with some of the sticky tobacco juice. That was a start, but the real difference for Covey was because of advice he received from two pitchers at Portland at the time, Harry Krause and Joe McGinnity, a future Hall of Famer who was known as Iron Man because in 10 seasons he pitched 3,441 innings, including five times when he pitched and won both games of a double-header.[6] They told Covey he needed to go to the drugstore and get alum to put in his mouth to create the best juice for the ball.

Just as he had when he threw stones at a tin can, Stan worked to perfect his new skill.

"I had as good control over the spitball as I had on my fastball," he recalled years later. "I could break it down, down and out or up. And I knew which way the ball's going. Just the wrist action, that's what makes the difference. I threw mostly overhand, some sidearm though, too."[7]

He also learned that when he was pitching into the wind, the ball would break down more than when he was pitching with the wind. So, when he arrived at a ballpark, he always would check which way the wind was blowing.

The period in baseball from around 1900 to 1919 was called the Deadball Era and was marked by the dominance of pitchers and an emphasis on defense. Most teams played "small ball," which meant putting the ball in play and using aggressive play and speed to score runs. A rule change early in the century made the first two fouls count as strikes, which also benefited pitchers. Previously, batters could foul off pitches until they got one they liked, and only balls that were bunted foul were counted as strikes. Plus, baseballs were used longer in games and softened the more they were used.[8]

The spitball was one more advantage for pitchers. Any change to the ball's surface could alter the balance and make it break in various directions. With the same ball used throughout most of the game, it was often marked and stained. As Covey learned, alum was the preferred substance used by spitball pitchers, but pitchers also found other ways to affect the ball's flight. Those included the shine ball, in which one side of the ball was rubbed against the uniform; the emery ball, in which sandpaper was used to scratch the ball; and the black ball, which was marked by licorice or tobacco juice.

But the secret to the spitball was more about how it left a pitcher's hand rather than adding a substance to the ball, according to Happy Jack Chesbro, who was one of the first great spitball pitchers. He had a 198-132 record during an 11-year career with the Pittsburgh Pirates, New York Highlanders, and Boston Red Sox between 1899 and 1909. He went 41-12 with New York in 1904 and was inducted into the Hall of Fame in 1947.

Chesbro learned the pitch by studying Elmer Stricklett, the father of the spitball. Stricklett played only four seasons in the majors and was 35-51 from 1904 to 1907, mostly with the Brooklyn Superbas.

In 1905, Chesbro, a right-hander, shared the secrets of the pitch:

It's an easy ball to pitch once you have acquired its secrets. I have never yet read an explanation of it that was anywhere near correct. I can make the ball drop two inches or I can make it drop a foot and a half.

The spit ball cannot be pitched so that it will drop toward a right-handed batsman. It can only be made to drop straight or to the outside. Of course, to a left-handed batsman it can be made to drop in toward him.

The thumb and thumb alone directs the spit ball. The saliva on the ball does not make it drop. In fact, the saliva does not affect the ball in any way. The ball must be moistened simply for the purpose of making the ball leave the fingers first and thumb last.

All curves and all balls leave the fingers last. By moistening the ball, the fingers slip off first and the thumb last. The thumb does the trick on the spit ball and does it well.

The ball is not hard on the arm. I pitched 51 games last season and my arm never bothered me. Speed must be used to make the ball effective, at least I always used speed, but the exertion is no greater than that of pitching fast straight ball. I can make the ball drop 10 feet from the plate, or two inches.[9]

The spitball was not the same as a wet ball or damp ball, according to Napoleon Lajoie, the great second baseman and manager at that time for the Cleveland team, which was called the Naps in his honor.

"The damp ball . . . can't be curved because it is wet all over, and the pitcher can't get a grip upon it," Lajoie wrote in 1905. "With the spit ball, it is different. The pitcher moistens only the spot covered by two fingers. If he wants to use another kind of delivery, all he has to do is grasp the ball in a dry place. . . .

"I am ready to admit that no style of delivery bothers me more; for there is absolutely no telling when and where the break is coming. I have frequently swung a foot and a half above the spit ball, as Jack Chesbro served it up to the batters last season, and that is pretty good testimony to its illusiveness, I am thinking, for I owe whatever success I have had in batting to the natural ability to watch the ball all the way up.

"Under control, the spit ball is the best thing in the pitcher's repertoire, but until it is under good control, it will seldom be used when a pitcher has a batter 3-2."[10]

Lajoie batted .338 during a 21-year career with the Philadelphia Phillies, Philadelphia Athletics, and Cleveland Indians, beginning in 1896. He was part of the second Hall of Fame class in 1937.

With his new pitch, the questions Stan had about his future at the start of the 1915 season were answered by the end of the year. He had a 17-17 record but was the best pitcher for Portland, which finished at 78-116 and in sixth place in the Pacific Coast League. His 2.67 earned run average led the team's starters, and he struck out 171 and walked 82 in 293 innings.

More important, the majors were taking notice. That fall, the American League needed a pitcher for an exhibition game against the National League in San Francisco and asked him to pitch.

A year that began with a lot of uncertainty for Covey ended with a lot of promise, and the spring of 1916 would bring more positive change for Stan and his family. On November 27, he was acquired by the Cleveland Indians and would head to spring training in a few months. Before he and Mary returned east from Portland, they welcomed their first child, William, on December 7, 1915.

Team photo of the 1913 Spokane Indians. Stan Coveleski is ninth from the left. (Photo from David Eskenazi Collection and used with permission.)

Team photo of the 1915 Portland Beavers. Stan Coveleski is fourth from the left in the front row. (Photo is in the public domain and was obtained from Wikimedia Commons.)

4

An emerging star

Stan and Mary returned with their new son to Shamokin, where Covey walked in the woods and ran to stay in shape for the start of spring training in New Orleans in 1916. As a pitcher, he had great control, but his newfound ability to throw a spitball had raised him to another level.

When Covey joined Cleveland in 1916, the Indians were a franchise that had declined. The team, which before 1915 was called the Naps in honor of star player Nap Lajoie,[1] had finished the 1914 season in last place in the eight-team American League with a 51-102 record. In 1915, the Indians finished seventh with a 57-95 record. The roster included outfielder Shoeless Joe Jackson, who had batted at least .338 in the previous five seasons, including .408 in 1911,[2] and shortstop Ray Chapman, who in 1920 would become the only player in major-league history to die as the result of being hit by a pitched ball.

The team's struggles created financial problems for owner Charles Somers. On August 20, with the team in sixth place with a 42-68 record, Somers traded Jackson and his $6,000 salary contract to the Chicago White Sox in exchange for $31,500 in cash, outfielders Bobby Roth and Larry Chappell, and pitcher Ed Klepfer.[3] Jackson led the White Sox to a World Series championship in 1917 and finished his 13-year career with a .356 average. But Shoeless Joe has been better remembered as one of eight players accused of accepting money from gamblers to throw the 1919 World Series, the infamous Black Sox Scandal, and who were banned from the league for life after the 1920 season.

Before the start of the 1916 season, wealthy railroad construction owner James "Sunny Jim" Dunn led a group of investors to purchase the Indians for $500,000. He quickly made several moves to improve the team, including purchasing first-baseman Chick Gandil from Washington. Then, in early April, Dunn made an even bigger move by acquiring star center-fielder Tris Speaker from the Boston Red Sox. Speaker had batted over .300 every season since he became a starter in 1909 and led the Red Sox to World Series titles in 1912 and 1915. He finished his 22-year career with a .345 batting average and still holds the career record with 792 doubles.[4]

When spring training began, the 1916 pitching staff was led by Guy Morton (16-15, 2.14 ERA in 1915) and Willie Mitchell (11-14, 2.82), and Klepfer was expected to add depth along with several others from the previous season.

"Two other pitchers reported to spring training with little or no fanfare," according to baseball author and historian Scott Longert in his book, *The Best They Could Be: How the Cleveland Indians Became the Kings of Baseball, 1916-1920*,[5] "Neither Stan Coveleski nor Jim Bagby (who was acquired from New Orleans of the Southern Association) got much press coverage when they showed up in February of 1916. Reports stated that Bagby had some skills as a pinch-hitter, while Coveleski had pretty fair control of his pitches. The odds of either one sticking with the varsity seemed to be remote at best."

Those odds changed significantly early in the season. But first, Covey needed a little help with the pitch that would define his career. When he arrived at spring training in New Orleans, manager Lee Fohl and coach Jack McCallister wanted to see Coveleski's spitball that they had heard so much about from the Portland team, but Covey couldn't throw it. In the January 9, 1922, *Plain Dealer* sportswriter Stuart M. Bell wrote the story headlined "Covey Almost Failed To Get Job Because He 'Lacked' Spitter," about how McCallister was a key to the start of Covey's career.

McCallister said Coveleski "appeared at the tribe's camp in New Orleans in 1916 dressed in a two-quart hat, a suit of clothes made to allow for development and a general air of somberness."

Fohl and McCallister were satisfied as they watched Covey throw his curve and fastball, but when they asked him to throw his spitter, the ball didn't break. The coaches didn't understand what had happened to Covey's pitch that he had thrown in the minors and asked why he couldn't throw it in the majors. Covey couldn't explain it, but the coach said he'd try to figure out what was wrong.

According to Bell's story, McCallister stood next to Covey as he pitched the next day. After several pitches with no break, McCallister said, "Don't hold the ball so tight, Covey." Stan wet the ball, loosened his grip, and threw to Fohl, who was catching. The ball broke and missed Fohl's mitt.

"From that day, he was one of the greatest spitball pitchers the major leagues have ever seen," Bell wrote.[6]

Cleveland played its home games at League Park at East 66th Street and Lexington Avenue. It was built in 1891 with wood, then rebuilt in 1910 with concrete and steel. The park originally had seating for 9,000, then expanded it to 21,400. Because of the streets around it, the right-field wall was only 290 feet from home plate, so a 40-foot-high wall was constructed. It was 375 to left and 420 to center.

The stadium was renamed Dunn Field after team owner Jim Dunn in 1921. The Indians played there for more than 50 years. Even after Cleveland Stadium opened in 1932, the Indians continued to play at League Park on weekdays, when smaller crowds attended, until 1947. It was demolished in 1951, but in 2014 the field was restored for youth games and recreation as part of the Baseball Heritage Museum.

In addition to the 1920 World Series, League Park was the site of Babe Ruth's 500th home run on August 11, 1929, and Addie Joss's perfect game for the Indians on October 2, 1908.[7]

Fohl's original plan was to use Coveleski as a relief pitcher. Covey made his first appearance for the Indians in the second game of the season in relief of Morton, who gave up four runs in the top of the eighth inning against the St. Louis Browns. Covey allowed two hits in a scoreless ninth in the Indians' 4-2 loss.

On April 17, Stan got his first start, pitching 12 innings in a 3-1 loss to the Detroit Tigers. He struck out six, walked two, and allowed 13 hits, although the great Ty Cobb was hitless against him in five at-bats, including a strikeout.

Newspapers originally billed the game as a matchup with Stan's brother Harry, who returned to the majors with Detroit in 1914, when he posted the first of three straight seasons with at least 21 wins. But Harry refused to pitch against his younger brother.

In the April 18 *Plain Dealer*, Henry P. Edwards termed Stan's performance brilliant for 11 innings and wrote:

> The advertised battle between the Coveleskie brothers failed to materialize. Manager Fold was willing that it be staged. Brother Stan of the Indians had a chip on his shoulder and dared Harry of the Tigers to knock it off, but brother Harry begged off, claiming he would be unable to do himself justice when pitching against a brother who was attempting to earn his baseball spurs.[8]

Years later, in an unsourced story, Harry explained that when he saw the newspaper that morning, he went to Tigers manager Hughie Jennings and said he wouldn't pitch against Stan, who was just breaking into the league.

The only time Stan and Harry appeared in the same major-league game was on September 4 of that year. Stan started for Cleveland but was knocked out after allowing five runs in ⅔ of an inning. Later in the game, Harry pitched ⅔ of an inning, allowing two hits in the Tigers' 7-5 win. Harry won 21 games that season with a 1.97 ERA in a career-high 324⅓ innings, but he developed arm trouble the following year. He was 4-7 the next two years and out of the majors early in 1918.

On April 26, nine days after the derailed faceoff against his brother, Stan earned his first win for Cleveland, 5-3, over the Chicago White Sox. He allowed two runs and nine hits in eight innings, struck out one, and walked one.

In his next start on May 1 in Detroit, Covey pitched a two-hit, 2-0 victory against the Tigers that was called after five innings, likely because of weather or darkness. Four days later, he pitched a complete game and beat the White Sox again, 3-2, allowing seven hits, striking out three, and walking three. The victory raised the Indians' record to 12-7 and moved them to percentage points behind the Washington Nationals (also known as the Senators) for first place in the American League. Cleveland stretched its winning streak to eight games and won 14 of 16 games to open a 2½ game lead in the league.

On May 18, Covey and Bagby combined to pitch the Indians to a 4-2 win over Washington and Walter "Big Train" Johnson, with Covey getting the victory. He also tripled and scored against Johnson, who in 1936 would join Ty Cobb, Babe Ruth, Honus Wagner, and Christy Matthewson as the first players elected to the National Baseball Hall of Fame.

On May 30 at Sportsman's Park in St. Louis, Covey was locked in a pitcher's duel with the Browns' Dave Davenport, each allowing one run through nine innings. Stan was not considered a good hitter, with a .159 lifetime average, but in the top of the 10th, he hit the only home run of his career. His inside-the-park homer also scored Ivan Howard and Steve O'Neill and gave Cleveland a 4-1 lead.

In the bottom of the inning, St. Louis scored three runs off Stan to tie it at 4. With one out, Covey gave up two singles and a double to score the first run. Ed Klepfer came in to relieve him and allowed the second run to score on a ground-out. The tying run, also charged to Covey, scored on an infield single by George Sisler. The Browns won in the 15th with a run against Klepfer.[9]

By the middle of June, Coveleski had an 8-3 record, and the Indians spent most of the month in first place and were in first or second until the middle of July. The team had another distinction that year as the first team to wear numbers, which they wore on their sleeves. They were removed after a few weeks, and there is no record of what number Coveleski wore during that time. In 1929 the New York Yankees became the first team to put numbers on players' backs permanently.[10]

On July 1, Covey pitched five innings of no-hit relief, and the Indians rallied to defeat the St. Louis Browns, 5-4, in 11 innings. On July 8, he pitched a complete-game 5-1 win over the Boston Red Sox, allowing five hits. Two days later, he earned a two-inning save against New York to move the Indians 1½ games behind the first-place Yankees.

Cleveland was in first place for the final time on July 12 after beating the Yankees, 6-3, with Covey earning his third save with 1⅓ innings of one-hit relief. The Indians faded after that, and an eight-game losing streak in the middle of August left them 8 games back and in sixth place.

They ended the season 77-77, 32-45 in the second half of the season, and finished 14 games behind the first-place Boston Red Sox.

There were reports that Coveleski had health problems during the season, including tonsilitis. On September 12, he lasted only ⅓ inning, giving up three runs on a walk and three hits, including a two-run homer by Ty Cobb in a 10-2 loss to the Tigers and dropping the Indians to .500 for the first time since late April. He didn't pitch again that season. *The Plain Dealer* reported that the team sent him home for the rest of the season because of sickness and overwork.

As expected, Speaker led the offense with a league-leading .386 average, but the surprising bright spots for most of the year were Coveleski and Bagby. Covey had a 15-13 record and a 3.41 ERA in 232 innings. Bagby was 16-17 with a 2.61 ERA in 279 innings. They would follow that with even better years.

Covey returned rested and strong in 1917.

There was a lot of uncertainty for baseball in the spring of 1917 because of labor issues in the sport and rumblings about the United States entering World War I. The Players Fraternity, founded by Dave Fultz in 1912 to protect players' rights and had more than a thousand members, filed four grievances, including one requiring owners to pay players while they were injured. The owners eventually agreed to that, and a threatened strike was averted.[11]

There was also concern that the season would have to be canceled if many players were required to report for military service. President Woodrow Wilson declared war against Germany on April 2, but Vice President Thomas Marshall wanted to see baseball continue to maintain the American way of life. Teams practiced military drilling during spring training to show support for the war effort.

As he had in 1916, Indians owner James Dunn made a big move to improve his team by acquiring pitcher Smokey Joe Wood from the Boston Red Sox. That was a risk because Wood's future in baseball was uncertain because of a sore arm that led him to sit out the 1916 season. Dunn believed Wood could return to his earlier form when he went 117-57 with a 1.99 ERA in eight seasons and led the Red Sox to the 1912 World Series title after winning 34 games, including 10 shutouts.

Dunn paid the Red Sox $15,000 for Wood. His move eventually would pay dividends but not in the way anyone expected. In the next three years with Cleveland, he pitched only 18⅓ innings in just seven games and had an 0-1 record and a 5.40 ERA. But Wood established himself as a good outfielder during his six years with the Indians, batting .297 in 1,718 plate appearances. Wood also became a good friend of Covey, spending time during the offseason at their hunting camp in Shohola Falls, about 45 miles east of Scranton in Northeastern Pennsylvania.[12]

Cleveland already had what would become a strong one-two pitching punch in Coveleski and Bagby, and in 1917 they gave a sample of what was ahead.

Unlike the previous season, the Indians weren't in first place for an extended time, but they did improve. They finished the year 88-66, 11 games better than 1916, and were third in the league, 12 back of the World Series champion Chicago White Sox.

Covey pitched a complete game in the season opener at Detroit on April 11 and beat the Tigers, 6-4. He allowed five hits, struck out two, and walked two. Five days later, he pitched a five-hit shutout against the St. Louis Browns, keeping the Indians in a first-place tie with the White Sox at 3-1. But Cleveland finished the month at 8-9

During May, Coveleski showed how dominant he could be. He won all five of his starts that month, including three shutouts, and allowed only one run in 44 straight innings. He started May with a string of 20 scoreless innings before giving up a run in the ninth inning on a sacrifice fly in a 7-1 win over Boston on May 17. He followed that with 24 straight scoreless innings before giving up two runs on three singles in the sixth inning of a 2-1 loss to the Red Sox on June 4.

Cleveland was 34-34 at the end of June but finished strong, going 19-6 in September.

On September 15, Covey was pulled after one inning when he gave up a run on a walk and two hits, but he was credited with the win after the Indians scored two runs in the top of the second and never again trailed in a 5-4 win. "He had nothing," sportswriter Henry P. Edwards wrote about Covey's short outing in *The Plain Dealer*. Coveleski came back four days later to beat the Yankees, 2-0, on a one-hitter, allowing only a single to Fritz Maisel leading off the seventh. In his final game of the season, he beat the A's, 2-1, allowing four hits in 11 innings in Philadelphia.

Covey had a 19-14 record, including a league-leading nine shutouts and 24 complete games, and a 1.81 ERA. In 298⅓ innings, he struck out 133 and walked 94. Bagby was 23-13, with a 1.99 ERA in 320⅔ innings, with eight shutouts, 26 complete games, 83 strikeouts, and 73 walks.

With one of the league's greatest players in Speaker and two rising pitching stars, baseball excitement grew in Cleveland. But the war was having an impact on baseball. By the end of the season, some players had received draft notices and headed overseas to join the fighting. That included pitcher Ed Klepfer, who had become a strong third pitcher behind Coveleski and Bagby with a 14-4 record and a 2.37 ERA. When the season ended, his career also ended because he missed the 1918 season while serving in the military and appeared in only five games in 1919 after returning from the war.

The 1918 season began with even more questions than the previous year. With the United States fully involved in the war, many players received their draft notices and were required to report for service. Public sentiment was that baseball should be shut down during the war. Some people, including owners, argued that baseball was important for public morale, but others believed the owners didn't want to cut off their revenue by suspending the season. Most minor leagues had stopped playing in 1917, but major-league baseball continued.

The war wasn't the only thing affecting the way of life in America. Early in the year, the Spanish flu surfaced, which resulted in restricted public gatherings and caused an estimated 675,000 deaths during the next two years in the United States.[13]

In Cleveland, there was another concern, although not life-threatening. Bagby believed he deserved a raise based on the previous season and announced he would hold out until he got one, but after a couple of weeks, an agreement was reached.[14]

The season was set to begin on April 16 at League Park in Cleveland with Coveleski starting, but heavy rains caused the game to be postponed. The same thing happened the next day. Finally, on April 18, Covey took the mound despite showers, and Cleveland defeated Detroit, 6-2. He went on to win his first four starts, all complete games, despite the Indians having a depleted lineup because of the flu. Combined with five straight wins at the end of 1917, he ran his winning streak to nine.

One of the most impressive games of Stan's career was on May 24, when he pitched 19 innings and beat the New York Yankees, 3-2, at the Polo Grounds. He gave up a run in the seventh on a homer by Ping Bodie, who also tied the game with a sacrifice fly in the bottom of the ninth to score Wally Pipp, who had tripled. Covey allowed 12 hits, walked six, and struck out four. He retired the Yankees in order in the second, fourth, fifth, 11th, 12th, 14th, 18th, and 19th innings and gave up only two hits in the final six innings. The Yankees went 0-for-9 with runners in scoring position and left 14 on base.

The game was played in three hours and forty-eight minutes.[15] There was no record of Covey's pitch count, but he likely threw more than 200 pitches. Smokey Joe Wood, now converted from a pitcher to an outfielder, hit two solo home runs for the Indians, including the game-winner in the top of the 19th inning. Allen Russell started and went seven innings for the Yanks. George Mogridge pitched 12 innings in relief and took the loss.

It was Covey's third extra-inning game in 10 days. On May 15, he had lost to the Philadelphia A's, 3-2, when he gave up two runs in the bottom of the 13th inning on a fielder's choice and a two-out single by George Burns. The A's had tied the score in the bottom of the ninth on a one-out home run by Tillie Walker. On May 19, he had lost to the Washington Nationals, 1-0, when he gave up a two-out hit to Clyde Milan in the bottom of the 12th.

"He pitched forty-four innings for an average of a little over fourteen innings per last three starts," Scott Longert wrote in his book *The Best They Could Be: How the Cleveland Indians Became the Kings of Baseball, 1916–1920*.[16] "The pitch counts are unknown; however, it is probable he threw in the neighborhood of five hundred pitches. By current standards, that number of pitches is unheard of. Coveleski did all this without a

31

whimper. He came from the school that taught simply taking the ball every three or four days and pitching until the game is over."

Covey was off to a great start, finishing May with a 7-3 record and a 1.34 ERA, but the remainder of the baseball season remained doubtful because of the war.

"Amid rising cries to halt play, owners made a concession for the 1918 season by reducing the schedule from 154 games to 140," Matt Kelly wrote in an article "On account of war" for the National Baseball Hall of Fame. "It was not enough, however, at least in the eyes of the military. On July 1, 1918, Secretary of War Newton D. Baker issued a 'work or fight' order, stating that all draft-eligible men who worked in 'non-essential' vocations must sign up for war-related work or risk being drafted for battle.

"The game was given a temporary pass, as government officials declined to recognize it as one of the 'non-essential' activities. But Newton's favor turned by the end of July when he publicly recognized that the unusually athletic men on the diamond should be using their talents to help their country on the battlefield. There was no getting around it: Baseball players would have to serve too."[17]

Players were receiving notices from their draft boards to find essential work or face enlistment. Sportswriter Henry P. Edwards of *The Plain Dealer* wrote on July 20 about the reaction of the Cleveland players to the "work or fight" order and the uncertainty about whether the season would end at that time. Speaker and Chapman planned to enlist in the Navy. "Steve O'Neill and Stanley Coveleskie may resume work in the coal mines of Pennsylvania," Edwards reported.

After much discussion, team owners and the government agreed that the regular season would end on Labor Day, and the World Series would start on September 4. Many of the players had left their teams to serve in the military.

In mid-August, the Indians were in second place, two games back of the first-place Red Sox, when they went to Boston for a three-game series. Babe Ruth pitched Boston to a 4-2 win in the first game, then Sad Sam Jones beat Coveleski, 6-0, in game two. Bagby beat Ruth in the series' final game, 8-4.

The Indians couldn't close the gap during the final two weeks and finished in second place with a 73-54 record after winning their final four games and eight of their last 12. Covey won three of those eight and saved another. Despite the challenges during the year, the Indians were heading in a positive direction. They didn't drop below .500 the entire season and led the league in attendance, drawing 295,515 fans to 60 games at League Park.

Coveleski finished with a 22-13 record, the first of his five 20-win seasons, and a 1.82 ERA. He pitched 25 complete games in 33 starts. In 311 innings, he struck out 87, walked 76, and allowed only two home runs. His record could have been better, but he lost three 1-0 games in which he pitched 12, 10, and 10 innings and lost another complete game, 2-0. Bagby was 17-16 with a 2.69 ERA, Guy Morton 14-8 and 2.64, and Fritz Coombe 13-7 and 3.06.

One of those 10-inning losses had another interesting note. On July 8 at Fenway Park, Covey and Sad Sam Jones were locked in a scoreless pitchers' duel in the first game of a doubleheader. In the bottom of the 10th, Covey gave up a one-out single to Boston's Amos Strunk, bringing Ruth to the plate. Ruth hit Coveleski's first pitch to him over the right-field wall to win the game with what now would be a two-run walk-off homer. But, according to rules at the time, when Strunk touched home plate, the game was over, and Ruth's hit was ruled a triple. The significance was that it would have given Ruth 715 career home runs instead of the renowned 714. Years later, there were efforts to change the ruling on Ruth's homer, but the rule at the time prevailed.[18]

When he was about 80, Covey recalled the pitch but not all the details of the game.

"I'm the one that made a hitter out of Babe," he told Shamokin radio personality Tom Kutza in a 1969 interview. "We were playing a game in Boston, and it was nothing-nothing, I think, in the 11th or 12th inning, and they had a man on third base, and Babe come up, and I know I brought one of the best spitballs I ever broke. It broke the wrong way, and he hit that darn thing out to right field, and this man came home from third. Here not so long ago, they were talking about you don't want to give him a home run, and this man at third base beat me. I give him credit for it.

"When Babe was through pitching, and the reporters in New York asked him who was the toughest pitcher he ever hit, he said, 'Coveleski.'"

Ruth hit only five of his 714 career home runs against Covey, all when the Babe played for the Yankees (Sept. 9, 1920; July 30, 1921; Sept. 26, 1921; July 19, 1924; April 30, 1926).

Boston went on to win the World Series over the Chicago Cubs in six games behind the pitching of Ruth and Carl Mays. Because of the shortened season, the Series wrapped up on September 11 and is the only Series to be played entirely in September.[19] The game also marked the first time "The Star-Spangled Banner" was played at a baseball game. Although the song would not be designated the National Anthem until 1931, it was played by a Navy training station band during the seventh-inning stretch, and fans and players sang in a show of patriotism.[20]

By then, many players were already serving in the military. Future Hall of Famers Ty Cobb, Christy Mathewson, and Tris Speaker were among those who enlisted. Others went to work in war-related industries, and there was concern that baseball might not return the next spring, at least with many of its stars.

There is no record of Covey serving in the military, but on his draft registration card signed on May 24, 1917, at age 26, he did not claim an exemption from the draft. It listed his "wife and child" as solely dependent on him for support, so it seemed likely that if he was not drafted and baseball shut down, he would have returned to work in the mines. His card listed his occupation as a baseball player for the Cleveland Baseball Club and his home address handwritten as "19 Lukfilder, Shamokin, Pa."

The best news of 1918 came two months after the World Series when a ceasefire was announced on November 11, signaling an end to the war. Americans looked forward to a return to normal life, and baseball looked forward to a full season in 1919, although the Spanish flu would continue to be a serious threat for at least another year.

Cleveland owner Jim Dunn liked the roster he had put together and was looking forward to a long-awaited championship, especially with Coveleski and Bagby in their primes and an offense led by Speaker and Chapman.

With players still returning from the war, team owners agreed to cut the season to 140 games. The Indians' season was scheduled to start on April 23 in Detroit, but just as in the previous season, the weather changed that. This time instead of rain, it was cold and snow. After two postponements, the teams played on April 25 despite high winds and cold. For the third straight season, Covey started the opener, but this time he lost to Detroit, 4-2. He gave up only two earned runs but allowed 10 hits in seven innings and was hurt by a couple of wind-aided hits. That was the only time the Indians were below .500 the entire season.

Six days later, Covey struggled in his next start in the home opener against Detroit, lasting only four innings and giving up six runs and 11 hits in an 8-1 loss. By the middle of May, he was 1-3 with a 3.25 ERA but had three saves. He did not lose again until the end of June, winning eight straight decisions and lowering his ERA to 2.23.

The Indians spent four days tied for first place during the month and stayed close until the end of June, when a six-game losing streak dropped them four games back. Fans were expecting more from the Indians, who won only 11 of their first 20 games in July and were slowly losing ground to the first-place White Sox. Covey pitched well during that stretch, going 3-1 with a no-decision. He beat the Browns, 11-1, the Yankees, 2-0, and the Nationals, 5-4, allowing two earned runs. All three were complete games. The loss was in relief. He lasted just 1⅓ in the no-decision.

Pressure from fans was mounting on the Indians and particularly on Manager Lee Fohl. On July 18, the Indians and Red Sox were tied at 3 when Cleveland scored four runs in the bottom of the eighth inning on a bases-loaded triple by pinch-hitter Joe Harris, who also scored on a wild throw to third. It was not enough. As fans started to leave League Field, Boston rallied in the top of the ninth against pitchers Elmer Myers and Fred Coumbe. The big blow was a grand slam by Babe Ruth, his second homer of the game, giving the Red Sox the lead, which they held for an 8-7 win.

After the game, Fohl went to see Dunn.

"I have failed to win the confidence of the fans although I have done my best to make the club a winner," Fohl told Dunn, according to Edwards' report in *The Plain Dealer*.[21] "I want you and Cleveland to have a winner, but if the fans think you ought to have someone else running the team, I think I should step aside."

Dunn accepted the resignation and named Speaker to manage the team. There had been speculation that Speaker would become player-manager since he had been acquired from Boston before the 1916 season.

The Indians were 44-34 and in third place when Fohl resigned. In his four-and-one-half years as the Cleveland manager, his teams were 327-310, but his only losing season in Cleveland was in 1915, his first year when the Indians were 45-79. After that, his teams won 55 percent of their games. But good was not good enough for the championship-starved Cleveland fans and Dunn. Fohl obviously was feeling the pressure.

Longert, in his book *The Best They Could Be: How Cleveland Indians Became the Kings of Baseball, 1916-1920*, wrote that Fohl said in an interview years later that he was looking for a way out as the manager and that the "change in managers was a mutual decision."[22]

The next day Coveleski pitched the Indians to a 7-4 win over the Red Sox to take the series, 3-1, and start the team on a four-game winning streak. The Indians finished 84-55, including a 10-game winning streak in September, but they couldn't catch the White Sox and finished in second place for the second straight season, 3½ games behind the American League champions. They were 40-21 under Speaker.

On September 12, Covey pitched a complete-game, 4-3 win over the Boston Red Sox. The game didn't mean anything in the standings, but it was a present for his son, Jack, who was born that day in Shamokin.

Coveleski led the Indians again with a 24-12 record and 2.61 ERA. He pitched 286 innings and had 24 complete games and four shutouts. Bagby was 17-11 with a 2.80 ERA, 241⅓ innings, and 21 complete games. George Uhle, a 20-year-old rookie, was 10-5 and would go on to win 26 games in 1923 and 27 in 1926 for the Indians.

Another pitcher of note was Ray Caldwell, who would be an important part of the 1920 team. But in 1919, he made headlines for something more striking.

Caldwell spent the first nine years of his major-league career with the Yankees before he was released, reportedly because of drinking issues. He was with the Red Sox for three months in 1919 but again was released. Speaker decided to take a chance on him.

On Sunday, August 24, the Philadelphia A's were in town for the second game of a three-game series, and Speaker gave Caldwell his first start under dark storm clouds. Caldwell, a spitball pitcher like Coveleski, responded with a strong performance, and the Indians led, 2-1, heading into the ninth. As the storm intensified, Caldwell got the first two outs on popups. Then a loud crack of lightning startled everyone. All the Cleveland players were OK except for Caldwell, who was lying on his back and knocked out after being struck. Players who approached him wondered if he was dead.

After a few minutes, Caldwell got to his feet and demanded the ball to get the final out. On his next pitch, Joe Dugan hit a hard grounder to third baseman Larry Gardner, who knocked the ball down, then picked it up and fired to first base in time to get the final out.[23]

Caldwell finished the season 5-1 for Cleveland after going 7-4 for Boston. That wasn't the only notable game for Caldwell in 1919. On September 10, he pitched a no-hitter and beat the Yankees, 3-0.

There would be more dark clouds ahead for baseball. The White Sox were favored to defeat the Cincinnati Reds in the World Series but wound up losing the best-of-nine series, 5-3. Questions immediately were raised that Chicago had thrown the series after some players were suspected of receiving payouts from gamblers. A year later, eight White Sox players, including outfielder Shoeless Joe Jackson and pitcher Eddie Cicotte were suspended from baseball for life. Jackson had a .356 batting average during 13 seasons and undoubtedly would have been elected to the Hall of Fame. Cicotte led the league in wins in 1919 with a 29-7 record and was 209-148 during a 14-year career with the Red Sox and the White Sox.

When the 1919 season ended, there was news that could directly affect Coveleski. To increase scoring, major-league owners were moving to outlaw the spitball.

1, Loudermilk; 2, Morton; 3, Klepfer; 4, Beebe; 5, Gandil; 6, Smith; 7, Bagby; 8, Bradley; 9, Houck; 10, Wambsganss; 11, Turner; 12, S. Coveleskie; 13, R. V. McRoy, Vice-Pres.; 14, Lee Fohl, Mgr.; 15, J. C. Dunn, Pres.; 16, Coumbe; 17, Howard; 18, Daly; 19, Evans; 20, Billings; 21, Graney; 22, Speaker; 23, Chapman; 24, O'Neill; 25, Kunkle; 26, Roth.
CLEVELAND AMERICAN LEAGUE TEAM, 1916.

Team photo of the 1916 Cleveland Indians. Stan Coveleski is second from the left in the second row. (Photo is believed to be in the public domain, but the source is unknown.)

League Park around the time when Stan Coveleski played there. (Photo from Detroit Publishing Company photograph collection at the Library of Congress. No known restrictions on publication.)

League Park around the time when Stan Coveleski played there. (Photo is in the public domain and was obtained from Wikimedia Commons.)

Tris Speaker. (Photo is from the Ernie Harwell Sports Collection, Detroit Public Library, and used with permission.)

Joe Wood. (Photo is from the Ernie Harwell Sports Collection, Detroit Public Library, and used with permission.)

Stan Coveleski, right, shakes hands with his brother Harry in 1916 when Stan was beginning his career with Cleveland and Harry was near the end of his career with Detroit. The brothers refused to pitch against each other. (Photo is believed to be in the public domain. It is not in the possession of the National Baseball Hall of Fame Library or Getty Images.)

Jim Bagby. (Photo is from the Ernie Harwell Sports Collection,
Detroit Public Library, and used with permission.)

Form 1   **1735**   REGISTRATION CARD 970 No. *20*

		Age, in yrs.
1	Name in full *Stanley Covaleski*	*76*
	(Given name) (Family name)	
2	Name address *19, Luckfelder Shamokin, Pa*	
	(No.) (Street) (City) (State)	
3	Date of birth *July 13 1890*	
	(Month) (Day) (Year)	
4	Are you (1) a natural-born citizen, (2) a naturalized citizen, (3) an alien, (4) or have you declared your intention (specify which)? *Natural Born*	
5	Where were you born? *Shamokin Pa., U.S.*	
	(Town) (State) (Nation)	
6	If not a citizen, of what country are you a citizen or subject?	
7	What is your present trade, occupation, or office? *Base Ball Player*	
8	By whom employed? *Cleveland Base Ball Co* Where employed? *Cleveland Ohio.*	
9	Have you a father, mother, wife, child under 12, or a sister or brother under 12, solely dependent on you for support (specify which)? *Yes. Wife & child.*	
10	Married or single (which)? *Married* Race (specify which)? *Caucasian*	
11	What military service have you had? Rank *None*; branch _____ years _____; Nation or State _____	
12	Do you claim exemption from draft (specify grounds)? *No*	

I affirm that I have verified above answers and that they are true.

Stanley Coveleski

(Signature of mark)

If person is of African descent, tear off this corner.

Stan Coveleski's World War I draft registration. (Image from Ancestry.com.)

Ray Caldwell. (Photo is from the Ernie Harwell Sports Collection, Detroit Public Library, and used with permission.)

Covey relaxing with a cigar and newspaper sometime during the 1910s.
(Photo is from the Steve Steinberg collection and used with permission.)

Stan Coveleski warms up during the 1919 season with Cleveland. (Photo is from the Steve Steinberg collection and used with permission.)

5

Tragedy and triumph

The 1920 season was a turning point for baseball. The Spanish Flu still was spreading, but the war was over, and Americans were looking for something to lift their spirits. Enter baseball. Major-league baseball, however, had its own problem—primarily the Black Sox cheating scandal of the 1919 World Series. That dark cloud would hang over for the entire 1920 season and impact the American League race by the end of the year.

The year brought significant changes in baseball. The Deadball Era ended with Babe Ruth emerging as the power-hitting face of the game. And the spitball was outlawed with a few exceptions. Owners moved to ban the "freak" pitches, giving more of an advantage to batters. They believed fans wanted to see more offense, and more fans meant more money for the owners.

Before 1920, there were no specific and enforced rules prohibiting the spitball and other alterations to the baseballs. That changed on February 9, 1920, when major-league baseball outlawed the spitball and other pitches where the ball was altered. Fortunately for Coveleski, he was among 17 players who were allowed to throw it for the rest of their careers under a grandfather clause. There was a lot of debate and speculation before that decision.

"It is a tricky and dangerous ball to control," claimed *Baseball Magazine* editor F.C. Lane, one of the leading opponents of the spitball, in "Should the Spitball Be Abolished?" in June 1919. "But once mastered, as only a few have been able to master it, it is all but unhittable."[1]

Among those who mastered it was Covey, and he saw no reason to ban it.

"I don't see why they took it out," he told Murdock in1974. "Ruth had to hit in all that stuff."[2]

Before the spitball ban, Henry P. Edwards wrote in a *Comment on Sports* column in the November 5, 1919, *The Plain Dealer*:

"Should (American League president) Ban Johnson induce American league magnates to abolish the spitball with the sailor, shiner, and other freak pitching systems, several clubs in the circuit would be hard hit.

"Chicago would find Cicotte and Faber of little value. Bernie Boland of the Tigers would be forced to use nothing but his curve and change of pace. Doc Ayers practically would be put out of business. Shocker of the Browns is a spitballer, while Sothoron roughs the ball and also throws a sailor. Of the Cleveland pitching staff, Coveleskie and Klepfer would be most affected. Covey also has a splendid fast ball and a good curve, but his splitter is his principal reliance. . . .

"It is believed, though, that if the league does take action in regard to the freak deliveries, there will be a clause allowing such spitball pitchers as are in the circuit to continue using that delivery. In other words, the rule will not be retroactive."[3]

That is what happened, as explained by baseball historian and author Steve Steinberg:

"There were a lot of things being done with the ball that were increasingly tampering. They would do the mud ball or the paraffin ball and, of course, the shine ball, where you would rub one side of the ball against your jersey. A lot of people back then were arguing that that couldn't possibly have anything to do with the flight of the ball. It got to the point there were so many devious things that were being done, and the owners wanted more hitting in the game. There was sometimes the argument that, unlike the other pitches, the spitball wasn't adding a foreign substance because it was part of your body.

"When they cleaned up the game before the 1920 season, the spitball was going to be banned flat out. Then they said, 'We've got to give these pitchers a year to transition, in all fairness, because they've been throwing the spitball. We'll give them one year, and they can learn how to throw a curveball again.' It was going to be banned a year later, but obviously, they were grandfathered in, and one of the reasons they were grandfathered in, there was a lobbying campaign. Stan doesn't strike me as a leadership guy. These guys were lobbying the owners and saying don't ban it. If you have a spitball pitcher and you ban it, you're giving away thousands of dollars of valuable merchandise.

"It just happened that Stan may be one of the big reasons—you can never know exactly why—why it wasn't banned. And the reason was, in the 1920 World Series, he was the hero, and to take away the best pitch of the hero, it was a big break for spitballers that the great spitballer was the hero of the World Series. Therefore, they grandfathered it."[4]

As a transition, when the 1920 season started, each team was allowed to designate two pitchers who could continue to throw a spitball. The following 17 pitchers were permitted to throw the spitball after the 1920 season:

American League
Doc Ayers, Detroit Tigers
Ray Caldwell, Cleveland Indians
Stan Coveleski, Cleveland Indians
Red Faber, Chicago White Sox
Dutch Leonard, Detroit Tigers
Jack Quinn, New York Yankees
Allen Russell, Boston Red Sox
Urban Shocker, St. Louis Browns
Allen Sothoron, St. Louis Browns

National League
Bill Doak, St. Louis Cardinals
Phil Douglas, New York Giants
Dana Fillingim, Boston Braves
Ray Fisher, Cincinnati Reds
Marv Goodwin, St. Louis Cardinals
Burleigh Grimes, Brooklyn Dodgers
Clarence Mitchell, Brooklyn Dodgers
Dick Rudolph, Boston Braves

Coveleski (1969), Grimes (1964), and Faber (1964) were spitballers from that group elected to the Hall of Fame. Grimes, who retired after the 1934 season and was the last to throw a legal spitball in the majors, was 270-212 in 19 years, mostly with Brooklyn. Farber was 254-213 in 20 years with the White Sox.

Covey believed his pitching ability went beyond the spitball. He pointed to his control and said sometimes he would go several innings without throwing a spitter, but he would go to his mouth before each pitch to keep the batters guessing.

"They're all good pitches if you pitch them in the right spot at the right time," he told Tom Kutza in 1969. "I used the spitball, but I didn't use it all the time. I had them looking for it."

At about the same time, Babe Ruth moved from pitching to playing every day in the outfield and, in the early 1920s, emerged as the first great power hitter. Before then, most of the better hitters choked up on the bat, slapped at pitches, and used speed to get base hits and score runs. Ruth stepped back in the box and swung for the fences.

Ruth was a very good pitcher early in his career with Boston, winning 23 games in 1916 and 24 in 1917. As his hitting ability developed, he was moved to the outfield so that he could play every day. In 1919, his last season with Boston, he hit 29 home runs, which was nine more than he had hit in his first five seasons combined. After his trade to the Yankees before the 1920 season, he pitched in only five games in his final 16 seasons. He finished his career with a pitching record of 94-46 and a 2.28 ERA in 10 seasons, but he changed the face of baseball by hitting 714 home runs during his 22-year career.

Baseball fans wanted to see offense, especially home runs, and baseball owners wanted to see those fans sitting in the ballparks.

Steinberg pointed to a comment in the New York *Evening Telegram* on August 27, 1920, by Walter Johnson, one of the greatest pitchers in the history of baseball:

"Hitting plays the most important role in a ball game. There is no getting away from the fact that the baseball public likes to see the ball walloped hard. The home runs are meat for the fans. 'Babe' Ruth draws more people than a great pitcher does. It simply illustrates the theory that hitting is the paramount issue of baseball."[5]

As good as Ruth was, the 1920 season belonged to the Cleveland Indians. For Stan Coveleski, the year would be the best of times and the worst of times. In Cleveland, baseball fever was raging, and fans would be happy when the World Series was over. But months before October, the season was marked by personal tragedy for Covey and the team.

The Indians had high expectations when they traveled to New Orleans in February for spring training, where Henry Edwards of *The Plain Dealer* filed this report on February 29:

"With one exception, the entire squad remained in action for the entire session. The exception was Coveleskie, who decided that twenty minutes were enough for him. Stan is of the opinion that he has been getting in shape too quickly in the past and thus runs the risk of going stale before the end of the season.

"'I want to be on the edge for the World's Series,' was the reason he ascribed for quitting the field so early."[6]

Covey believed he could get into pitching shape quickly because he remained in shape throughout the year. He showed that early in the season by winning his first seven games.

In the April 14 season opener at League Park, he beat the St. Louis Browns, 5-0, on a five-hitter, striking out seven and walking two. He also went 2-for-3, driving in the game's first run with a single in the second inning and leading off the fourth with a double. He followed that by defeating the Tigers, 11-4, Browns, 11-3, White Sox, 3-2, and Tigers, 9-3.

On May 3, he was sent to Cleveland from Detroit because he had suffered what seemed to be a serious ankle injury, but Dr. M.H. Castle, the team physician, determined it was a sprain and Covey could rejoin the team in Chicago for a five-game series. He won the opener, 3-2, on May 5, allowing one earned run in nine innings, and four days later won the series finale, 4-3, for his seventh straight win. It also moved the Indians into sole possession of first place in the American League for the first time with a 14-6 record, one-half game ahead of Boston. The next day Bagby beat the Browns, 7-3, to raise his record to 6-0, giving the Indians' two star pitchers 13 of the team's first 15 wins.

Covey's first loss was to the Yankees on May 15. He allowed only two hits through seven innings in the first time he faced the Yanks with Ruth in their lineup. Boston had traded Ruth before the season, but it wasn't Ruth who did the damage this day. Number seven hitter Ping Bodie led off the eighth with a single, then with one out, opposing pitcher Jack Quinn hit a homer to deep right field for what would be a 2-0 Yankees win.

Four days later, Covey beat the Yanks, 5-0, on a six-hitter. On May 23, he lost to the Athletics, 2-1, when he gave up a two-out, two-run double to Joe Dugan in the top of the eighth. Both runs were unearned because of an error by second-baseman Bill Wambsganss.

On the morning of Friday, May 28, Coveleski arrived at League Park to prepare for the opener of a four-game series against the White Sox. Sitting in the locker room dressing for the game, he was called to the executive office. He was given a telegram informing him that his wife Mary had died.[7]

Mary, 28, had been ill for several years, but Covey had no indication that he was about to lose her. While he was in Cleveland playing baseball, she had remained in Shamokin to care for their two young boys—William, 4, and Jack, 8 months—with help from other family members.

Covey immediately left for Shamokin. Like Stan, she was a native of Shamokin, a daughter of Joseph and Anna Shivetts, and lived with them at 27 Vine Street when she died. The cause listed on her death certificate was pulmonary tuberculosis, complicated by influenza, and her name was spelled Kovalewski. She was buried on May 31 in St. Stanislaus Cemetery.

Notice of Mary's death was posted in the May 29 edition of *The Plain Dealer*:

> The flag at League Park yesterday was at half-mast in respect to Mrs. Stanley Coveleskie, who died at her home in Shamokin, Pa., yesterday morning. Stanley, the tribe's star pitcher, received the notice at noon. He had expected to pitch yesterday afternoon but, upon receiving the news, made preparations to leave for home. Mrs. Coveleskie, who has been ill for nearly three years, was not thought to be in a critical condition, and her death came as a great surprise to Stanley. In addition to her husband, she leaves two young children. The players and President Dunn

made arrangements for floral tributes for the funeral, which will be held either tomorrow or Monday. Covey expects to return to Cleveland late next week.[8]

Stan remained in Shamokin for about a week, then returned to Cleveland, leaving his two sons to be cared for by Mary's 20-year-old sister, Frances.

On June 6, Covey started the first game of a doubleheader against St. Louis, but understandably he wasn't at his best, allowing 11 hits in seven innings and losing 6-2. Four days later, he beat the Athletics, 7-2, and on June 14, he allowed five hits and no earned runs in a 7-1 win over the Yankees. Both were complete games.

On June 13, there was another concern. After the game, a 14-0 loss to the Yankees, catcher Steve O'Neill received word his wife had given birth to twin girls. A few hours later, he got a telegram telling him to immediately return home to Minooka, Pennsylvania, near Scranton, because his wife was ill. He ran to the station to catch the first train. After a few days she recovered, and he rejoined the team on June 20.

Covey was 3-3 in June, then returned to his old form, going 6-2 in July. Among those games was a 5-3 win over the Philadelphia A's on July 14, as reported in *The Plain Dealer*:

Stanley Coveleskie lost and then won his own games against the Athletics here this afternoon, and the tribe grabbed off its second straight, 5 to 3.

The Pole allowed the Mackmen to paste his slants for three runs in the first inning, and it looked as if the pastime were pickled. One would guess that from the shouts of the leather-lunged fanatics that it was all over. But the stout-heartedness of the Indians and Stanley had not been reckoned with.

In the eighth, when the statistics were knotted, the Pole came through with a base hit, and the deciding marker came over the pan. But that was not all of Stanley's batting prowess. He ripped out a double at the start of the third, and he later scored on Tris Speaker's slap to left for a base.[9]

After the first inning, the Pole was master all the way. In the first, his spitter was not working at par. The Quaker City gang slaughtered his shoots for three doubles and a single, but thereafter only four hits were allotted the trailers.

The Indians also had an excellent July, going 22-10 to take a three-game lead over the Yankees. Speaker was batting .418, and all the other starters except second-baseman Bill Wambsganss (.245) were over .300. August would not be as good for the team or Coveleski.

Covey was 2-5 in August, but some of that was a lack of run support. He allowed 16 earned runs in 57 innings—a 2.53 ERA—but the Indians scored only 11 runs in those seven games, including five runs in his five losses.

From May 8 to August 21, the Indians were in first place in the American League for all but six days. But the team struggled in August, going 11-16, including a five-game losing streak from August 9-14. But there was worse news than baseball losses during the month.

On August 16, when the Indians opened a two-week road trip to New York, Boston, Philadelphia, and Washington, they were 0.004 percentage points behind the White Sox, and the Yankees were a half-game back. There were dark clouds, and a light rain fell when the game against the Yanks started at the Polo Grounds. Coveleski started for the Indians and Carl Mays for the Yankees in a matchup of team aces.

Mays was a hard-throwing, side-arm pitcher known for pitching inside and was not well-liked in the league. Cleveland took the lead on a solo homer in the second inning by Steve O'Neill and added two in the fourth on an error and a sacrifice fly by Coveleski.

Ray Chapman led off the top of the fifth. He had bunted in his two previous at-bats, resulting in a sacrifice and a double-play. The rain had stopped when he stepped into the batter's box, but the skies still were dark. Mays' first pitch to Chapman came in high and inside. Chapman never moved, and the ball hit his left temple with such force that it caromed onto the field. Mays, believing the ball had been bunted, picked it up and threw it to first base. But the crack he had heard was from the ball hitting Chapman's skull, not his bat.

Chapman fell to the ground unconscious. Players and several doctors rushed to the plate, and a few minutes later, Chapman responded. He began to walk toward the clubhouse but collapsed again and had to be carried off the field. He was transferred to St. Lawrence Hospital, where initial indications were that the injury might not be as serious as originally thought, but doctors soon determined his skull was fractured and operated. Again, there seemed to be some hope, but in the early morning hours of August 17, Chapman died.

The popular player, who became the only player in major-league history to die from a pitched ball, had married Kathleen Daly before the season, and they were expecting their first child. She would never recover from the loss and, eight years later, committed suicide. A year later, their eight-year-old daughter, Rae Marie, died from measles.

When Chapman was carried from the field that day, players were shaken but didn't know his condition would be fatal, so the game continued. The Indians added a run in the fifth on an RBI single by O'Neill for a 4-0 lead. In the bottom of the ninth, with two outs, Covey gave up a two-run double to Ping Bodie and an RBI single to Muddy Ruel to cut it to one run but got pinch-hitter Lefty O'Doul on a grounder to shortstop to end the game.

There was speculation that Chapman never saw the pitch from Mays, possibly a combination of the dark skies and a dark baseball, the result of a decision by owners to continue to use discolored baseballs longer during games to save money.[10]

There was a lot of angry reaction from players toward Mays, who said the pitch was an accident and expressed remorse. Mays was questioned by authorities but wasn't charged. American League president Ban Johnson, following the funeral for Chapman, also declined to act against Mays, as reported by Henry Edwards in the August 21 edition of *The Plain Dealer*:

> No official action against Carl Mays, by whom the ball was thrown that killed Ray Chapman, will be taken by President B.B. Johnson of the American league. The case is ended as far as Johnson is concerned.

"I could not conscientiously attempt to make any trouble
for Mr. Mays," said President Johnson yesterday afternoon, "after
listening to the wonderful sermon preached by Father Scullen.
But it is my honest belief that Mr. Mays never will pitch again.
From what I have learned, he is greatly affected and may never
be capable, temperamentally, of pitching again. Then I also know
the feeling against him to be so bitter among members of other
teams that it would be unadvisable for him to attempt to pitch
this year at any rate."[11]

The article went on to report:

The Indians were grievously affected on their return to
Cleveland yesterday morning, and while only three of the squad
actually broke down, it was only the exercise of all their willpower
that others kept from following suit.

Secretary Walter McNichols fainted on the train soon after
leaving New York. While Jack Graney and Steve O'Neill gave way
on arriving at the Daly residence yesterday. Jack Graney became
so hysterical Nap Lajoie, former king of second basemen, who was
present, took him by force and, placing him in his automobile,
drove him out into the country while the funeral was in progress.

Tris Speaker was another who was unable to attend the
funeral. He had a nervous breakdown yesterday morning and was
ordered to bed by his physician.

An attached article from wire services reported:

Carl Mays, the Yankee pitcher, whose pitched ball killed Ray
Chapman, the Cleveland shortstop, today was reported in a
nervous breakdown which confined him to his home, preventing
his appearance in the traffic court on a charge of speeding.

Mays did come back to pitch nine more seasons. He shut out the
Tigers on 10 hits a week after hitting Chapman. He went 8-2 the rest

of the season and finished 26-11, but he didn't pitch against the Indians for the rest of the year. The next season he was 27-9, including a 6-3 win on May 16 in Cleveland. He finished his 15-year career in 1929 with a 207-126 record for the Red Sox, Yankees, Reds, and Giants.

Mays maintained for the rest of his life that he had not intentionally thrown at Chapman.

"I ain't saying much about Mays," Coveleski said in 1974 when discussing the incident in a recorded interview with Eugene Murdock. "He was a hard man to hit against, and I'll tell you why. He had a darn good fastball and a good curve, and both underhanded. You didn't know which way it was going to break. I don't think he tried to hit him. But at that time, if you see a fellow getting too close in there, you'd fire under his chin."[12]

It would be 50 years before helmets became mandatory in professional baseball.

Chapman batted .278 during his nine-year career, all with Cleveland, and along with Tris Speaker, was considered a leader of the team. Losing him not only took a key player from the team but a close friend of many players, including Speaker and O'Neill. There were reports of a fight between those two before the funeral. Nerves were frayed, and the season started to slip away for the team.

After Chapman's death, the grieving Indians lost seven of their next nine games. August was by far their worst month of the season, and they dropped into third place, 2½ behind the White Sox and 1½ behind the Yankees. Harry Lunte, who replaced Chapman on August 16, continued as the starting shortstop for the next 19 games, going 13-for-65.

It seemed a lifetime ago that the Indians had left on the two-week road trip, but they managed to win their final three games in Washington before heading home for the next 24 days. Perhaps they saw an opportunity to honor their lost friend by focusing on the game they all loved, and things changed for the Indians, who wore black arm bands to honor Chapman and won 22 of their next 28 games. During the run, rookie Walter "Duster" Mails was 7-0, Bagby 6-2, Covey 5-2, Caldwell 3-2, and George Uhle 1-0. In Coveleski's two losses, the Indians scored one run.

Mails joined the Indians on August 29 from the Pacific Coast League. The left-hander was wild in his September 1 debut, lasting only one inning, but finished the season strong with a 1.85 ERA in 63⅓ innings and six complete games and pitched Cleveland to a 1-0, three-hit victory in Game Six of the World Series. He had another good year in 1921, going 14-8, but he could not handle the taunting from opposing teams[13] and was out of baseball in 1926, finishing his seven-year career with a 32-25 record.

On September 7, 21-year-old Joe Sewell was called up from New Orleans of the Southern Association. He made his major-league debut on September 10, when he popped out as a pinch-hitter in the fifth inning. Two days later, he went 2-for-4, including a triple in the second inning for his first hit.

No one expected Sewell to fill Chapman's shoes in 1920, but he went on to have an excellent career. He finished the 1920 season with a .329 average in 22 games. In his 14-year career with Cleveland (11 seasons) and the Yankees, he batted .320 and was the toughest player in major-league history to strike out, according to the Hall of Fame. In 7,132 at-bats, he struck out only 114 times. He was inducted into the Hall of Fame in 1977.

On September 17, Coveleski pitched a complete-game 9-3 win over Washington, and the Indians moved into sole possession of first place and stayed there for the remainder of the season. It was the third game during a season-high seven-game winning streak. The Indians finished September with four straight wins and a 1½-game lead over the White Sox, who won 10 of their final 11 in the month.

Any hopes Chicago had of catching the Indians ended on September 28 when a Chicago grand jury indicted eight players for their role in the cheating scandal during the 1919 World Series, and the seven players still with the White Sox were suspended by the team. The players were acquitted the following year on August 2, but the next day baseball commissioner Judge Kenesaw Mountain Landis banned them from the sport for life. Those banned were pitchers Eddie Cicotte and Lefty Williams, outfielders Shoeless Joe Jackson and Hap Felsch, and infielders Swede Risberg, Buck Weaver, Fred McMullin, and Chick Gandil, who supposedly was the ringleader and who retired after the 1919 season.

The fix was a black eye for baseball and became known as the Black Sox scandal. Baseball had a lot of work to regain its fans' trust. Babe

Ruth's emergence as a home-run hitter was key to that. But the first to emerge from the shadows were the Cleveland Indians in the fall of 1920. They clinched the American League championship on Oct. 2 with a 10-1 win over Detroit. It was Bagby's 31st win of the season.

Cleveland finished 98-56, two games ahead of the White Sox and three ahead of the Yankees. The Browns were a distant fourth, 21½ back.

Coveleski finished the regular season 24-14 with a 2.49 ERA, 26 complete games, and 315 innings. He struck out 133, the only time he led the league in strikeouts in his career. Bagby was 31-12 with a 2.89 ERA, 30 complete games, and 339⅔ innings. Caldwell answered the need for a third strong starter, going 20-10 in 237⅔ innings, despite a 3.86 ERA. It would be his last good year. He was out of the major leagues after going 6-6 in 1921. The team batted .303, led by Speaker's .388 average.

A team that had started the season with so much hope and endured unimaginable difficulties won its first American League pennant, but there was even better news ahead, especially for Coveleski.

Ray Chapman. (Photo is part of the Ernie Harwell Sports Collection, Detroit Public Library, and used with permission.)

Joe Sewell. (Photo is part of the Ernie Harwell Sports Collection, Detroit Public Library, and used with permission.)

The 1920 Indians team wearing black armbands in memory of Ray Chapman. Stan Coveleski is fourth from the left in the front row. (Photo is part of the Ernie Harwell Sports Collection, Detroit Public Library, and used with permission.)

6

World Series hero

Looking back, much of the 1920 season was a nightmare for Coveleski and the Cleveland Indians. Deaths, slumps, and internal conflict were among the things that threatened to derail their championship hopes, but somehow the players pulled together and were about to see their baseball dream come true.

The World Series originally was scheduled to begin on October 5 in Cleveland, but Indians owner Jim Dunn, seeing an opportunity to bring more fans into League Park, was installing additional bleachers, and the project wasn't completed. So, he asked the National Commission to open the best-of-nine series at Ebbets Field, home of the National League champion Brooklyn Robins. It was agreed that the Series would open with three games in Brooklyn, followed by four in Cleveland and two in Brooklyn if all nine games were needed.

The Robins, also called—and soon to be permanently named—the Dodgers (short for Trolley Dodgers), had won the National League pennant with a 93-61 record, seven games ahead of the New York Giants. They took control in the middle of September, winning ten straight games in seven days, including three doubleheaders, and wrapped it up at the end of the month by taking three of five from the Giants. They were led by outfielder Zack Wheat (.328), first-baseman Ed Konetchy (.308), and pitcher Burleigh Grimes (23-11, 2.22 ERA).

Baseball needed to recover from the tragic Chapman death and the Black Sox scandal, and the 1920 Series would produce some special moments: an unassisted triple play by Bill Wambsganss, the only one in World Series history, and a grand slam by Elmer Smith, the first in Series history. But the real star would be the former coal miner from Shamokin with three complete-game wins.

Game One
Cleveland 3, Brooklyn 1
October 5, Ebbets Field

Coveleski was manager Tris Speaker's obvious choice to start Game One. He had not pitched in five days, although that didn't matter to Covey because he was used to pitching a lot of innings with little rest. He pitched a career-high 315 innings during the regular season and averaged more than 288 innings pitched during his first five seasons with Cleveland, including the 19-inning game in 1918.

"I wasn't scared," he told Tom Kutza in 1969. He believed they would win if his team scored a couple of runs.

Brooklyn manager Wilbert Robinson selected left-hander Rube Marquard to start, hoping for an advantage against the Indians' left-handed batters, including Speaker. Marquard, a Cleveland native, had spent his first eight seasons pitching for the New York Giants, including three straight years with at least 23 wins. In 1920, the eventual Hall of Famer was 10-7 with a 3.23 ERA. The Robins' ace, Burleigh Grimes, another future Hall of Famer, had pitched three days earlier against the Giants.

The game started at 2 P.M. with cold temperatures and gusty winds, which Damon Runyon described in the next day's edition of *The Plain Dealer* as "a stiffish north wind that blows out of a cold gray sky" and "a cold day, much too cold for baseball." The Indians, who were in new blue uniforms and wore black armbands in memory of Ray Chapman, scored their first run in the top of the second after first baseman George Burns hit a high popup that was helped by the wind and dropped in behind first base for a single. When he saw shortstop Ivy Olson wasn't covering second, Burns took off for second base. First-baseman Ed Konetchy's throw to second rolled toward the boxes behind third base, and Burns raced home for a 1-0 lead.

The Indians added the deciding run when Steve O'Neill doubled to left field, scoring Smokey Joe Wood, who had walked and advanced to third on a single by Joe Sewell.

Meanwhile, Covey retired the first nine Robins batters. On his first pitch of the game, Olson flied out to Wood in right field. Covey threw a called third strike to Jimmy Johnston and got Tommy Griffith on a grounder to shortstop.

Cleveland added a run in the top of the fourth on a two-out, line-drive double to right by O'Neill, scoring Wood, who had doubled to left. Cleveland didn't get another hit for the rest of the game, but the three runs were enough for Coveleski.

Olson led off the fourth inning with the Robins' first hit, a single to center. After a groundout, Griffith singled to put runners on first and second, but Covey got fly-ball outs by Zack Wheat to left and Hi Myers to deep right to end the threat. The Robins threatened again in the sixth when Olson singled with one out and reached second on a sacrifice, but Covey got Griffith on a grounder to the mound.

Brooklyn scored its run in the seventh when Wheat led off with a double, moved to third on a grounder to shortstop, and scored on a grounder to first base. The Robins threatened again in the eighth when a single and walk put runners on first and second with one out, but Covey shut down the rally on a popup to third and a groundout to second. The first out was a long drive by Ernie Krueger to deep left-center that center-fielder Speaker ran down, making a spectacular catch to save a likely triple that could have changed the game's direction.

"It does not look as if he has a chance to get the ball," Runyan wrote about the play. "The Brooklyn fans are cheering wildly. Now, still going at full speed, Speaker's hands drop down, and he pitches himself a bit forward. He has the ball. He makes the catch just below his knees. It is a play rather typical of Speaker, say the experts. The Brooklyn cheers stop abruptly."[1]

Runyon wrote about Coveleski: "He is a spitball pitcher, the best in his own league. He moistens the ball with saliva, putting it up to his mouth before he delivers it as if he were eating an apple."

The front-page, all-capped banner headline in the next day's *Plain Dealer* was "COVEY WINS OPENER FOR INDIANS" and was followed by the deck heads "Big Pitcher, Aided by Speaker and O'Neill, Defeats Brooklyn, 3-1" and "Polish Hurler, Under Leaden Skies and With a Stiff Breeze Blowing Over Ebbets Field, Takes Dodgers' Measure; Cleveland Stars Scoring in Second, Getting Two, and Draws One More in Fourth; Marquard Sent From Box."

Covey's line was five hits, one run, three strikeouts, and one walk. Marquard lasted five innings, giving up all three runs and five hits, striking out four, and walking two.

After the game, Speaker said: "The result of the game goes to show that I was not boasting when I contended that Cleveland would display just as good pitching as Brooklyn. They would have us believe that Brooklyn has the real pitching market cornered.

"It is my belief that the pitching in the American league is every bit as good as that in the National, and our batting average of .302 was deservedly earned.

"Coveleskie pitched excellent ball today. With the wind blowing as hard as it was, he worked under a handicap, but he delivered in the pinches, and that is what counts. He never was nervous. It was just a ball game with him. He pitched a typical Coveleskie game."[2]

Game Two
Brooklyn 3, Cleveland 0
Oct. 6, Ebbets Field
The weather improved for Game Two, and so did the Robins. The pitchers with the best regular-season records for their teams faced off—Jim Bagby, who was 31-12 with a 2.89 ERA for the Indians, and Burleigh Grimes, who was 23-11 with a 2.22 ERA for the Robins. Grimes, who, like Coveleski, was among the last spitballers, had his pitches working to near perfection.

Brooklyn took a 1-0 lead in the second when Zack Wheat doubled with two outs to center field, scoring Jimmy Johnston, who had singled, stole second, and reached third on a groundout. The Robins added a run in the third on a double to right by Tommy Griffith, driving home

Grimes, who had led off with a single. Their final run came in the fifth when Ivy Olson singled, moved to second on a groundout, and scored on a two-out single by Griffith. Cleveland left ten on base and went 0-for-8 with runners in scoring position. Their best opportunity was in the eighth when they loaded the bases on three walks, but Grimes got out of it with a grounder to second.

"We could not hit with men on bases, and Brooklyn had two batters who could," manager Tris Speaker said after the game. "I think that is the best reason I know for explaining why we lost."[3]

Grimes scattered seven hits, struck out two, and walked four. Bagby lasted six innings, giving up seven hits, a walk, and two earned runs.

Game Three
Brooklyn 2, Cleveland 1
October 7, Ebbets Field

With the Series tied, Cleveland's Ray Caldwell was given the start in Game Three against Sherrod Smith, who was 11-9 with a 1.85 ERA during the regular season, splitting time between starting and relieving. It proved to be a good move by manager Wilbert Robinson. Smith limited the Indians to three hits and an unearned run in a complete-game 2-1 victory.

Caldwell struggled with control from the beginning. Ivy Olson walked to lead off the bottom of the first and moved to second on a sacrifice bunt. An error by Joe Sewell at shortstop put runners at first and third, then Zack Wheat singled to left for the first run, and Hi Myers singled to right for the second. That was the end of the scoring for the Robins and the end of the game for Caldwell after just one-third inning. Duster Mails came on in relief and allowed just three hits in 6⅔ innings. George Uhle allowed one hit in the ninth.

Cleveland's run came in the fourth when Tris Speaker doubled to left field, then raced around to score when the ball got past Wheat for an error. Cleveland's only other hits were singles by Steve O'Neill in the fifth and eighth innings, but both innings ended with double-plays. The damage had been done early, and Brooklyn held on for a 2-1 Series lead as the teams headed to Cleveland.

As a team, the Indians were not hitting. Their .165 batting average would have been worse if not for O'Neill, who was 5-for-10 (.500), and Speaker, who was 3-for-11 (.273).

The Indians looked forward to their trip home, where they hoped things would improve.

James Lanyon, the sporting editor of *The Plain Dealer*, prophetically wrote in the next day's edition: "They are behind in this annual competition for the championship of the baseball world. They are behind the Brooklyn Dodgers one game but are set for the greatest display of advancing from the rear that ever was displayed on the diamond."[4]

Game Four
Cleveland 5, Brooklyn 1
October 9, League Park

After a travel day, the Series resumed at League Park in Cleveland. Brooklyn was feeling confident, but everything wasn't perfect for the Robins. A Cleveland police detective had arrested pitcher Rube Marquard for scalping tickets. Police did not want the arrest to be an excuse if Brooklyn lost the Series, so they released him with plans for a court appearance after the Series.[5]

The Indians were glad to return home, where they expected their offense to awaken. More important, Speaker had Coveleski ready to start Game Four.

"We have just begun to fight," Speaker told *The Plain Dealer's* Henry P. Edwards on the day before the first World Series game ever to be played in Cleveland. "You know they had us down a few times during the American league season, but they could not keep us down. Brooklyn has us down now, but it cannot keep us there."[6]

Leon Cadore, who was 15-14 with a 2.62 ERA during the regular season, started for Brooklyn. On May 1 of that year, he and Joe Oeschger of the Boston Braves locked up in a 26-inning marathon, the longest in major-league history. The game was called because of darkness, with the score tied at 1.

Before Game Four, Billy Evans wrote in *The Plain Dealer*:

Coveleskie, because of the fact that he uses the spitball almost exclusively, places a severe strain on his arm. He is at his best when he gets a four-day rest between starts. If he works Saturday, and I am positive of this, he will have had only three days' rest. For that reason, some of the critics fear he may not be up to his usual standard.

However, I have no fear on that point. I watched Covey carefully in the opening game, and he never seemed to exert himself. He worked easily throughout, and his control was such that he wasted very few balls. Perhaps a half dozen balls were hit real hard, but his support came to his rescue every time.

Coveleskie has something in reserve, aside from what he showed in the opener, and I look for him to turn in one of his very best games. That means the Brooklynites will have an argument on their hands.[7]

Evans' words came true. As he did in Game One, Coveleski didn't allow a baserunner in the first three innings. And the Indians' bats did come to life. They jumped on Cadore for two runs in the first on a walk by Bill Wambsganss, a single by Speaker, an RBI single by Elmer Smith, and a sacrifice fly by Larry Gardner. They threatened again in the second when singles by Joe Sewell and Steve O'Neill knocked out Cadore. Al Mamaux came in to strike out Coveleski and end the threat with a double play when Charlie Jamieson hit a fly ball to shallow center, and Sewell was caught off second base.

Cleveland continued the attack in the third when Wambsganss and Speaker led off with singles to drive out Mamaux. Marquard came in to pitch for the Robins, and George Burns greeted him with a two-run single to left field, giving the Indians a 4-0 lead.

In the top of the fourth, Brooklyn got its only run when Jimmy Johnston singled to left, and Tommy Griffith doubled to right-center. Coveleski scored Cleveland's final run after singling with two outs in the fifth inning against reliever Jeff Pfeffer for his only hit in the World Series. Covey moved to second on a wild pitch, reached third on a single by Joe Evans, and scored on a single to shortstop by Wambsganss.

The Indians had 12 hits, all singles, against the four Robins pitchers. Speaker, Wambsganss, and Sewell led the way with two each. O'Neill was intentionally walked twice. Coveleski scattered five hits, struck out four, and walked one.

Speaker knew how important it was for his team to avoid a 3-1 hole in the Series. After the game, he told *The Plain Dealer*:

> They can talk about their 'money pitchers' all they want, but when they make up the lists of the pitchers who have performed wonderfully and done all we asked of them, they will have to include Stanley Coveleskie, who won his second game of the series today,
>
> He not only is the best spitball pitcher in the country, but he also is one of the best pitchers in the land regardless of style of delivery. He was an iceberg on the rubber today. I don't believe he realized there were 27,000 crazy ugs there this afternoon and that a defeat might hurt our chances more than I would like to admit.
>
> He pitched just as calmly as though it were an exhibition game against a bush league club.[8]

Henry P. Edwards wrote about Coveleski:

> His exhibition yesterday practically was a duplicate of his first victory as he again permitted five hits, walked one, and let the Robins send one man across the plate.
>
> "Score two runs for me, and I will win the game," said Covey to his teammates in the clubhouse prior to the game. "Perhaps one run will be enough, but I can work easier if you get two for me."[9]

In an article headlined "Covey's Iron Arm Starts Series All Over Again" in the October 10 *Plain Dealer*, Damon Runyon described Coveleski as too much for Brooklyn: "Coveleskie's spitball acts like a thing bewitched when he works in this series. It seems to break away from the bats of the Brooklyn men. He is a mighty pitcher."

"Cleveland richly deserved to win this afternoon's contest," Evans wrote in *The Plain Dealer*. "The pitching of Coveleskie was perfect. In addition, the Indians displayed a rushing attack that completely smothered four members of the much vaunted Brooklyn staff."[10]

After the game, Speaker told Covey to be ready for Game Seven.

"He said, 'Looks like you'll have two days of rest, then right back for the next one,'" Coveleski recalled in 1974. "I said, 'OK.' I could pitch every day. It made no difference to me."[11]

Game Five
Cleveland 8, Brooklyn 1
October 10, League Park

There were three more games scheduled in Cleveland, which meant the Indians could clinch the Series at home. One more loss and the teams would return to Brooklyn to finish the best-of-nine Series. Two more wins for the Indians and Covey would start Game Seven with a chance to clinch. Even if the teams split the next four games, Tris Speaker almost certainly would have come back with Covey in a deciding Game Nine, again after two days off. Cleveland players and fans not only wanted to win their first championship, but they also wanted to celebrate it in their home city.

This one was memorable in terms of offense and defense. Jim Bagby and Burleigh Grimes matched up again, but the result was much different this time. Cleveland jumped on Grimes for four runs in the bottom of the first. Charlie Jamieson, Bill Wambsganss, and Speaker led off with consecutive singles to load the bases. Elmer Smith then homered to deep right field for the first grand slam in World Series history.

The Indians scored three more runs in the fourth. After Jimmy Johnston singled and Steve O'Neill was intentionally walked, Bagby homered to deep center, the first home run by a pitcher in Series history. That chased Grimes, whose spitball wasn't working. He lasted just 3⅓ innings and gave up seven runs on nine hits. They took an 8-0 lead in the fifth against reliever Clarence Mitchell when Speaker reached second on a throwing error by third-baseman Jack Sheehan, moved to second on a single by Smith, and scored on a single by Larry Gardner. They could have had more, but Mitchell got Joe Sewell on a foul popup to third and, after another intentional walk to O'Neill to load the bases, got Bagby on a grounder to shortstop.

Bagby was in trouble several times and gave up 13 hits, but the Cleveland defense bailed him out. The sixth was the only inning when Bagby didn't allow a baserunner.

In the second, Ed Konetchy hit a one-out triple to center field. Pete Kilduff then hit a fly ball to left field, but Jamieson caught the ball and threw home to catcher O'Neill to get Konetchy for a double play to end the inning. The Robins hit three singles in the third but failed to score, largely because of a 5–4–3 double play. In the fourth, O'Neill threw out Hi Myers at third when he tried to advance from first on a wild pitch.

The biggest defensive play was in the fifth when Wambsganss executed the only unassisted triple play in World Series history. Kilduff and Otto Miller opened with singles, then Mitchell hit a line drive to second-baseman Wamby, who moved to his right and caught the ball. The runners were moving, and Wamby stepped on the second-base bag to get Kilduff, then tagged Miller, who was running to second. It happened so quickly that fans didn't realize what they had witnessed and were momentarily silent before erupting into cheers.[12]

Brooklyn finally scored in the ninth on consecutive one-out singles by Zack Wheat, Myers, and Konetchy, but Bagby stranded two runners in scoring position to end the game and give Cleveland an 8-1 win and a 3-2 Series lead. That was the last run the Robins scored in the Series.

"We gave future teams playing in the world's series something to shoot at," Speaker said after the game. "The series is not over, but I am confident that we will win."[13]

Game Six
Cleveland 1, Brooklyn 0
October 11, League Park

Based on his strong showing in relief in Game Three, Duster Mails was selected by Tris Speaker to start Game Six for the Indians. Sherry Smith, who had won that game by limiting Cleveland to one run on three hits, started again for Brooklyn. Smith again limited the Indians to one run, but Mails was even better this time.

The brash left-hander, who started his career in 1915 with a few appearances for Brooklyn before being sent to the minors for three years, told *The Plain Dealer* before the game: "Brooklyn will be lucky to get a foul off me today. If Spoke and the boys will give me one run, Cleveland will win."[14]

His request was answered, and his prediction came true. The Indians scored the only run of the game in the sixth inning when Speaker hit a two-out single to left field and was driven in with a double to left by George Burns. Mails allowed only three hits, struck out four, and walked two. The only time he was in serious trouble was the second inning, when the Robins loaded the bases with two outs on a single by Ed Konetchy and errors by shortstop Joe Sewell and third-baseman Larry Gardner on ground balls. But Mails got Smith on a fly ball to short center field to end the inning.

"All I can say about Walter Mails is that he is a wonderful pitcher," Speaker said. "I do not know of a better left-hander in the business. His fastball is something that no hitter can fool with. He has been a great find for us and will be one of our best pitchers next season. It was a tough spot he was in this afternoon, the toughest of the Series, and yet he came through. He was given the acid test if ever a young player was and proved 18 carats fine."[15]

The victory gave Cleveland a commanding 4-2 lead in the series. After the game, Speaker wouldn't commit that Coveleski would start Game Seven, but most fans expected he would.

An unbylined article in *The Plain Dealer* claimed there was "little doubt" Cleveland would win the series on October 12: "To win three straight, Brooklyn must beat Coveleskie, Bagby, and Mails. It cannot be done—not by Brooklyn."[16]

Zack Wheat, the Robins' captain, was just as confident his team would win three straight.

"We'll hit from now on," he said. "If Coveleskie pitches tomorrow, we'll drive him out of the box, despite his two victories."[17]

Game Seven
Cleveland 3, Brooklyn 0
October 12, League Park

It was no surprise when Coveleski took the mound for Game Seven after two days of rest. In a matchup of future Hall of Famers, Burleigh Grimes, who had started Game Five but lasted only three innings, started for Brooklyn. The game, which was played in unseasonably nice weather for Cleveland in October, 72 degrees and clear skies,[18] drew 27,525 fans, the largest crowd of the Series.

Brooklyn threatened first in the third inning. Grimes singled to short left field, then moved to second when Ivy Olson was safe on an error by shortstop Joe Sewell. But Covey got out of it when Jack Sheehan's groundball hit Olson for the second out, and Tommy Griffith flied to right field to end the inning.

Zack Wheat led off the Robins' fourth with a drive off the right-field wall, but Elmer Smith played the bounce perfectly and fired the ball to Bill Wamby at second base to get Wheat. Covey got Hi Myers on a bunt to third and Ed Konetchy on a fly ball to deep left field.

Cleveland scored its first run in the bottom of the inning. Singles by Larry Gardner and Doc Johnston put runners on first and third. After Sewell flied out to short left field for the second out, Cleveland looked to score on a double steal. When Johnston took off for second, catcher Otto Miller, recognizing the play, threw the ball to Grimes. Johnston stopped several feet before second base, and Grimes thought he could get the out at second, but he threw wildly, allowing Gardner to score easily from third.

The Indians made it 2-0 in the fifth when Speaker tripled to right field, scoring Charlie Jamieson, who had singled and stole second. The final run scored in the seventh. Steve O'Neill doubled to deep center field. Coveleski attempted to sacrifice, but Grimes threw to third to get O'Neill, who stayed in a rundown long enough for Covey to reach second. Jamieson doubled to score Coveleski.

Stan retired the Robins in order in the second, fifth, sixth, and eighth innings. Their only other threat was in the seventh when Konetchy singled with two outs and went to second on a ground-ball error by Sewell, his second of the game and sixth of the Series. But Covey ended the rally when he got pinch-hitter Bill Lamar to ground out to second.

In the ninth, Griffith flied out to left field, but Wheat kept Brooklyn's hopes alive with a single to center field. Covey got Myers and Konetchy on ground-ball force outs to shortstop to end the inning, the game, and the Series.

The page-one banner headline in the next day's *Plain Dealer* read, "CLEVELAND WINS WORLD'S SERIES."

In the final game, Coveleski threw only 90 pitches and gave up five hits with one strikeout and no walks. Grimes went seven innings and allowed three runs, two of them earned, on seven hits. He struck out two and walked four.

James H Lanyon, the sporting editor of *The Plain Dealer*, wrote: "Stanley Coveleskie—the pride of Cleveland, Shamokin and the remainder of the U.S.A.—yesterday defeated the Brooklyn Dodgers for the third time in the 1920 world series. And out and above the other chaps who have distinguished themselves in this annual fall baseball jewel, the Shamokin spitter stands as the hero of heroes."

Lanyon continued: "He went to the mound, and he pitched and pitched. He pitched his head off. An (stet) when the game had been brought to a most successful (stet)—from a Cleveland standpoint—he had shut out the champions of the National league. He had won for Cleveland the baseball championship of the world. To whom, then, shall we turn as the great hero of the list of heroes of the 1920 series? All together, boys—Stanley Coveleskie.

"The name Coveleskie has lived long in baseball annals. May it continue."[19]

An unbylined article in *The Plain Dealer* was headlined "Covey Pitches Only 90 Balls" and "Analysis Shows Indian's Control Was Perfect."

"Only twenty-one of Coveleskie's efforts were called balls, twenty-five were strikes, eight foul strikes, and three fouls," the article reported. "He retired twelve men on flies, and sixteen sent out easy grounders. Five hits were made by Brooklyn.

"Coveleskie pitched only four times in the fourth inning."[20]

If there had been a most valuable player award for the Series, it clearly would have been given to Coveleski. In his three complete-game wins, he allowed 15 hits and two earned runs in 27 innings for a 0.67 ERA, struck out eight, and walked only two. O'Neill (7-for-21, .333), Speaker (8-for-25, .320), Smith (4-for-13, .308, 5 RBIs), and Jamieson (5-for-15, .333) led the Indians' offense.

Wheat, who had written a daily column for *The Plain Dealer* giving the opposing team's view during the World Series, praised Speaker and Coveleski: "Looking back over the series, the work of Coveleskie stands out as the feature surmounting any stunt plays such as triple plays or home runs."[21]

In a column that was part of a newspaper advertisement for Wm. Taylor Son & Co., Ann Sawyer, a clothing buyer for the department store, wrote:

> After that cheery little 3 to 0 score yesterday, what do you think Superintendent of Schools Jones (stet) said:
>
> "Next week, at 4 o'clock, I'm going to let every school boy in town stand attention and throw the largest spit-ball he can find—in honor of Stanley Coveleskie, our spit-ball king!"
>
> But that isn't all. Felix Hughes and all the other music teachers in town declared:
>
> "Of course, yesterday put Mr. Coveleskie on the pedestal with Paderewski—as one of the two greatest Polish *players*. Paderewski may have composed a famous minuet. But Coveleskie certainly made a hit with his famous *third straight Polka!*"[22]

Billy Evans, an umpire and sportswriter, wrote an insightful article about Covey that also shared some rare comments by the Silent Pole. Evans wrote in the October 13 *Plain Dealer*:

> Speaker did a great thing for baseball when he sent his pitching star to the mound despite the fact that he had only two days of rest. He tempted fate in so doing because had Coveleskie

been beaten, Brooklyn would have come back with renewed confidence on its home grounds.

I understand Tris put it entirely up to Coveleskie. He wanted Covey to start if his arm felt right . . . and although he was far from feeling right, he accepted the task without a murmur.

That is the way Coveleskie does things. No matter how many errors his teammates make behind him, he never gets peeved. Umpires never know that he is in the ball park as far as making a protest is concerned. He simply does his work in a cold, calculating manner and accepts the breaks of the game as they come.

It is a rather remarkable thing for a pitcher who uses the spitball as much as Coveleskie to work three such games inside of eight days. Throwing the spitball is a sever (stet) strain on the arm. After the game, I dropped down into the Cleveland dressing room to congratulate Stanley on his great work.

"You pitched a great game today, Covey," I remarked. "In fact, no pitcher ever worked three better games in a world's series."

A broad grin spread over his face as he gave me a hearty handshake. Coveleskie talks but little. He is the sphinx of baseball. However, he was feeling mighty good when I talked to him, and deservedly so, and I feel sure he made the longest speech of his life in response to my congratulations.

"I guess I did look fairly good out there today, but I didn't feel much that way. Two day's rest isn't enough for a fellow who uses the spitter as much as I do. My arm felt dead. It didn't seem to me as if my spitter had the usual snap to it.

"However, I felt sure that if I could get the Brooklyn team to keep hitting at my spitter, I would be able to beat them. I wasn't, that is, not at my best, even though I did shut 'em out. Speaker wanted me to start if I felt able, so I started.

"Don't overlook Steve O'Neill when talking about my pitching. It is great to pitch to a fellow like O'Neill. Seldom do I shake my head at his sign, yet I did it once this afternoon when Wheat was up, and he hit the hardest drive of the game.

"I thought I might slip over a fast one. He made an even
faster one out of it when he connected. I am glad we were able to
finish it in seven games and glad I was able to do my part."[23]

Years later, when Covey talked about the Series, he remembered
a calm reaction compared to the way players celebrated in later years:
"Pitched that game and won it and walked back alone to the clubhouse.
And nobody said a word except maybe 'Nice game, Covey.' Just another
ball game."[24]

Championship-starved baseball fans in Cleveland, however, were
excited. A celebration was held the next day at Wade Park, and at times
the enthusiastic crowd got out of hand. The page-one banner headline
in the October 14 *Plain Dealer* was, "25,000 IN JAM AT BASEBALL
JUBILEE".

Fans wanted to get close to the players, including Coveleski, who
were on a platform. Covey had been late arriving for the program and
was cheered when he approached the stand. People in the back of the
crowd pushed forward, crushing those in the front. Some people were
pushed into a lagoon at the park, but no serious injuries were reported.

The Plain Dealer also reported in the October 14 edition that each
player's share for winning the World Series was $3,986.84. In the story,
Henry Edwards wrote that most players were heading to their homes:
"Joe Wood will go back to his New Jersey home and spend the winter
felling trees, getting the logs to market and hunting and fishing. Stanley
Coveleskie will hustle back to Shamokin and then join Wood on a hunting trip."

The article noted: "While the Indians were receiving automobiles,
watches, and watch-fobs, one set of gifts was sort of overlooked. Every
member of the Indians was presented with a black leather belt with a
handsome silver buckle, engraved with the player's initials."[25]

After the season, fans started a fund to show their appreciation to
Covey. As of October 17, $1,205 had been raised, but it was not noted if
it would be presented to him as a gift or cash. He also was given a watch
charm by Polish friends in Cleveland. *The Plain Dealer* reported: "On the
face is a baseball insignia, while the reverse bears a Polish White Eagle,

made of platinum and studded with diamonds. The center lead has a baseball diamond on the one side and an inscription on the other."[26]

Only 13 pitchers have won three games in a World Series. When Coveleski became the eighth member of that group in 1920, two previous three-game winners were there to witness it: Bill Dinneen was the umpire at first base, and Joe Wood was a reserve outfielder for the Indians.

Pitchers who won 3 games in a World Series:

YEAR	PITCHER	TEAM	GAMES	IP	ERA	RESULT
1903	Bill Dinneen*	Boston Americans	2, 6, 8	35	2.06	Won in 8
1903	Deacon Phillippe**	Pittsburgh Pirates	1, 3, 4	44	3.07	Lost in 8
1905	**Christy Mathewson**	New York Giants	1, 3, 5	27	0.00	Won in 5
1909	Babe Adams	Pittsburgh Pirates	1, 5, 7	27	1.33	Won in 7
1910	Jack Coombs	Philadelphia Athletics	2, 3, 5	27	3.33	Won in 5
1912	Smokey Joe Wood*	Boston Red Sox	1, 4, 8	22	4.50	Won in 8
1917	**Red Faber***	Chicago White Sox	2, 5, 6	27	1.67	Won in 6
1920	**Stan Coveleski**	Cleveland Indians	1, 4, 7	27	0.67	Won in 7
1948	Harry Brecheen	St. Louis Cardinals	2, 6, 7	20	0.45	Won in 7
1957	Lew Burdette	Milwaukee Braves	2, 5, 7	27	0.67	Won in 7
1967	**Bob Gibson**	St. Louis Cardinals	1, 4, 7	27	1.00	Won in 7
1968	Mickey Lolich	Detroit Tigers	2, 5, 7	27	1.67	Won in 7
2001	**Randy Johnson**	Arizona Diamondbacks	2, 6, 7	17⅓	1.04	Won in 7

Bold – Hall of Fame
*Also lost one game in the series
** Also lost two games in the series

Front pages of *The Plain Dealer* reporting Stan Coveleski's three World Series victories. (Images from Genealogybank.com)

Stan Coveleski warming up during the opening game of the 1920 World Series. (Photo is from the Steve Steinberg collection and used with permission.)

Bill Wambsganss. (Photo is from the Ernie Harwell Sports Collection, Detroit Public Library, and used with permission.)

7

A last hurrah

When the 1920 World Series ended, there still were questions about the future of spitball pitchers. Although the pitch was banned after the season, baseball officials agreed to allow 17 well-known spitballers to continue using the pitch for the remainder of their careers. Covey likely had a lot of influence on that decision because it wouldn't have been fair to eliminate the best pitch of the hero of the World Series.

By 1921, Babe Ruth had established himself as the star of baseball because of his power hitting. During his first four seasons with Boston, when he was primarily a pitcher, Ruth totaled nine home runs. For the next three seasons, as he became an everyday player, he surpassed his previous career total in each year, hitting 11 in 1918 (20 career total), 29 in 1919 (49 total), and 54 in 1920, his first season with the Yankees.

He didn't do as well in those years against Coveleski. At the start of spring training in 1921, Henry Edwards of *The Plain Dealer* summarized Ruth's success against the Cleveland pitchers. In four years, Ruth batted only .268 against Covey, going 11-for-41, with one home run, two doubles, one triple, 22 walks, and seven strikeouts.[1]

But 1921 would be the year Ruth and the Yankees gave the first hint of the dynasty that was to come. They won their first American League pennant that year, one of six in the 1920s. They lost in the Series to the New York Giants in 1921 and 1922, then won their first World Series by beating the Giants in 1923. During the next five decades, the Yankees would play in over half of the World Series, winning 19 of 26.

1921 SEASON

Cleveland's fortunes were not as successful. The Indians would not win another American League pennant for 28 years and would claim only one other World Series title when they beat the Boston Braves in 1948.

On February 27, *The Plain Dealer* reported on the opening of spring training: "Stan Coveleskie arrived with a big diamond decorating the third finger of his left hand, the gift of friends and fans of Shamokin, his hometown. Stan has been taking life easy since the world series. After hunting for a few weeks with Joe Wood, Elmer Smith, and other Indians in their camp near Wood's home, Covey went back to Shamokin to rest."[2]

In 1921 there still was baseball excitement in Cleveland, and the Indians had another great year, but they couldn't quite match their success of the previous season, finishing 94-60 and in second place, 4½ games behind the New York Yankees. They were in first place for all but two days from April 28 until the end of August, but they finished the season, losing three of four to the Yankees and three of four to the White Sox as part of a season-ending 21-game road trip. They won their season series with every team in the league except the Yankees, who took 14 of 22.

Much of the Indians' hopes for the season was because of the return of pitchers Coveleski, Jim Bagby, Ray Caldwell, Guy Morton, and Duster Mails.

Coveleski almost duplicated his 1920 season. He went 23-13 with 28 complete games out of a league-leading 40 starts and matched his previous year with 315 innings. It was his fourth straight season with at least 22 wins, but his ERA jumped to 3.37 from 2.49 the previous year, and his 341 hits allowed were 57 more than in 1920. He also was the league-leading fielder among pitchers with a .992 fielding average, with 23 putouts and 108 assists in 43 games.[3]

Bagby slid to 14-12 with a 4.70 ERA, and Caldwell was 6-6 with a 4.90 ERA. Mails was 14-8 with a 3.94 ERA, and Morton was 8-3 with a 2.76 ERA.

A brief bright spot was Allen Sothoron, another of the grandfathered spitball pitchers acquired from the Boston Red Sox during the season. Other teams suspected Sothoron of doctoring the baseball, including throwing the shine ball and emery ball.[4] He had won 20 games for the St. Louis Browns in 1919 but in 1921 was 1-4 with St. Louis and Boston before joining the Indians, where he went 12-4 with a 3.24 ERA, perhaps benefitting from being on the same staff as the greatest spitballer in the league. It was his last successful season.

"The spitballer never again enjoyed a season such as 1921," Charles F. Faber wrote in an article for the Society for American Baseball Research biography project. "He is destined to be remembered mainly for a one-liner penned by Bugs Baer: 'Allen S. Sothoron pitched his initials off yesterday.'"[5]

Coveleski again started the season opener. The St. Louis Browns scored a run in the third without a hit because of a walk and two of three errors in the game by shortstop Joe Sewell. Covey gave up only five hits in seven innings, but the Browns bunched four of those in the sixth—three doubles and a single—for three more runs. The Indians tried to come back in the ninth, scoring two runs on a home run by Elmer Smith and three singles, but a double play ended the threat and gave St. Louis a 4-2 win.

The next day the Browns took a 9-2 lead after three innings against Duster Mails and two relievers before Cleveland rallied against Sothoron, who still was with St. Louis, and two relievers for a 12-9 win. Covey pitched the final two innings for a save.

In the first two weeks of the season, the Indians' offense was the story. They averaged more than 7½ runs per game, and the team moved into first place with a 10-4 record.

On May 16, Carl Mays returned to pitch at League Park, now called Dunn Field, in Cleveland for the first time since he threw the ball that resulted in the death of Ray Chapman. The Yankees won, 6-3.

Henry Edwards described the scene in the May 17 *Plain Dealer:*

> It was in silence that Mays strode to the box in the first inning. Close to 10,000 fans, nearly every one of them an Indian partisan, sat in the stands. They displayed their sportsmanship by refraining from any effort to remind the New York pitcher of the great blow his pitch dealt the Cleveland club last year.

On the other hand, there were a few who followed the lead of the New York players and baseball writers and joined in the faint applause that greeted Mays when he first went to bat.

There was but one expression of hostility. That was in the seventh inning when Mays led off at bat for the Yankees. Pitcher Mails of the Indians, who was dubbed with the nickname 'Duster' when he played for Brooklyn because of using tactics made famous by Mays, threw the first ball near to his rival's head. Mays dropped to avoid being hit, and the crowd greeted the act with applause for Mails and jeers for Mays.

Mails also threw the next ball too close to Mays for comfort, and Carl swung in self-defense and raised a foul to Johnston.[6]

After the loss in the opener, Coveleski won nine of his next 11 starts, including three wins over nine days during the Indians' eight-game winning streak in late May. Cleveland opened a four-game lead over the Yankees in early June and was in first place until the beginning of September, except for two days in August.

Coveleski was 21-9 at the end of August, but on September 1, he left the game in Detroit after three innings when he pulled a ligament in his right side while pitching. Losing Covey would be a big blow for the Indians, especially with Bagby struggling. Bagby had suffered a similar injury the previous year and missed two weeks. Stan returned to Cleveland to be examined by Dr. H.M. Castle, team physician, who termed the length of Covey's absence "indefinite."[7]

Nine days later, Covey was back on the mound. He limited St. Louis to two runs and seven hits in seven innings, but the Indians managed just three hits against Urban Shocker and lost 2-0 in the first game of a doubleheader, dropping them two games back of the Yankees. The next day, there was more bad news when Speaker, who was batting .369, suffered a knee injury.

On September 14, Coveleski beat the Athletics in Philadelphia, 8-5, allowing just two earned runs and striking out eight. He also drove in two runs in the fifth inning with a single after Steve O'Neill was intentionally walked to load the bases with one out.

Speaker returned to the starting lineup after missing almost two weeks, but the Indians stayed in the race while he was out, winning eight of 11.

Covey lost his next three starts, including two against the Yankees, who won three of four in the teams' final series. He pitched poorly in just one—an 8-7 loss to the Yankees that dropped the Indians two games back with four games to play. Covey lasted just 2⅓ innings and gave up four runs, including Babe Ruth's 57th homer of the season in the first inning. In his final start, Covey beat the White Sox, 3-2, to keep the Indians two games back, but they lost their final two games to the White Sox, while the Yankees won their last three.

1922 SEASON
At the start of spring training in 1922, there were a lot of questions about the Indians' pitching staff: Could Jim Bagby bounce back? Could Allen Sothoron, Duster Mails, and Guy Morton match their previous season? There was no question about Ray Caldwell. The pitcher who had finished a game in 1919 after being struck by lightning was suspended for breaking training rules late in the 1921 season and was released when the season ended. He didn't play again in the majors.

The one constant was Coveleski, who announced that he planned to use his spitball more this season. "From now on, I'm a spitball pitcher and nothing else," he said.[8]

Coveleski led the team with a 3.32 ERA, but his record fell to 17-14.

The answers to the questions about the other pitchers were mostly no. Bagby finished 4-5 with a 6.32 ERA. He was waived after the season and signed by Pittsburgh, where he went 3-2 with a 5.24 ERA in 21 games in 1923. His nine-year career ended just three years after he won 31 games. Mails was 4-7 and .5.28 in 1922, and Sothoron was 1-3 and 6.39. Of the group, only Morton had some success, going 14-9 with a 4.00 ERA. George Uhle, in his fourth year with the team, had the first of his three seasons with 22-plus wins, going 22-16 with a 4.07 ERA.

Cleveland got off to a fast start, winning its first five games, but the Indians finished May at 7-8. Their only month above .500 was July when they were 20-12, including a 12-game winning streak. Coveleski won four of those 12 games during a 14-day span.

For the first time since 1917, Coveleski didn't start the opener. Because of the cold weather on April 12, manager Tris Speaker was concerned about the effectiveness of Covey's wet delivery and started Morton, who pitched the team to a 7-4 win. Covey didn't start the next day but pitched seven innings in relief of Uhle for a save.

Coveleski's first start was on April 17, but the game was called because of rain in the fourth inning after Covey retired the first 10 St. Louis batters. His first decision was the Indians' first loss of the season. He gave up 12 hits and six runs in seven innings in a 15-1 loss to St. Louis on April 19.

Covey was 8-11 at the end of June but then won six straight in July to raise his record to 14-11. On July 15 in Philadelphia, he beat the Athletics, 2-0, on a three-hitter for his third win in eight days. The game had another significance, as reported in *The Plain Dealer* the next day: "Jackie Coveleskie, 3, son of the Indian ace, took his first train ride this morning when he came over from Shamokin to visit his distinguished father and see his first big league ball game. Jackie was quite the king of the Indian bench with a big cap askew over his eyes. Covey went to Shamokin tonight for a Sunday holiday."[9]

Coveleski won three of his next six starts, but his season ended in late August because of an intestinal problem[10] or an injury suffered during an East Coast road trip.[11]

By the end of August, the Indians were 13 games behind the eventual league champion Yankees. They finished the season 78-76 and in fourth place, 16 games back.

Ownership of the Cleveland team also changed during the 1922 season. Jim Dunn, who had spent money to acquire players to improve the team, became ill with the flu and died on June 9, 1922. His wife, Edith, became the owner, and Ernest Barnard became the president and ran the team. Edith sold the team in 1927.[12]

1923 SEASON
Coveleski struggled at times during the next two seasons, and fans began to wonder if his career was almost over. In 1923, he showed signs of his old dominance and led the league with a 2.76 ERA and five shutouts, but

he was 13-14 that year and 15-16 the next, the only losing seasons in his 14-year major-league career.

He started the 1923 season opener and gave up 10 hits and five runs in 7⅓ innings. He pitched well until the eighth inning when the White Sox rallied for four runs to take a 5-4 lead before the Indians came back to win in the bottom of the ninth on RBI singles by right-fielder Homer Summa and shortstop Joe Sewell.

Covey won his next three starts, pitching 27 straight scoreless innings. He shut out the Tigers, 1-0, on five hits in 10 innings and scored the game's only run when, with two outs, he was hit by a pitch, moved to second on a walk, and scored on a throwing error. He then beat the White Sox, 3-0, on eight hits, and the Tigers again, 4-2, allowing both runs in the bottom of the ninth.

The Indians ended April 10-3, in first place by 1½ games over the Yankees, but that changed quickly. They went 12-14 in May and fell seven back of New York. Although they finished the season a respectable 82-71, they were in third place, 16½ games behind the Yankees, who won their first World Series championship.

In Covey's first start in May, he was hit on the pitching wrist by a line drive by St. Louis catcher Hank Severeid in the second inning. He continued to pitch, even though his wrist swelled and every throw was painful. He blanked the Browns until the sixth inning when Cedric Durst homered. In the seventh, he gave up four unearned runs on a three-run shot by Ken Williams, followed by another solo homer by Durst. Covey finished the inning but lost the game.

After that, Covey had an up-and-down season. He was 4-3 in May but 1-5 in June. On May 20, he shut out the Red Sox, 1-0, on six hits and drove in the only run in the bottom of the fifth with a two-out single. He lost a 4-3, 13-inning decision to the Washington Nationals and Walter Johnson on June 18, then on June 23, he lasted one inning when the muscles in his right shoulder tightened. He made his next start on June 29 but lost to the White Sox, 5-4, giving up four earned runs in seven innings.

If there was an impact from the wrist injury, Covey didn't let it show and continued to pitch. In July, he was 5-3, but 0-3 in August. On July

15, he lasted 1⅔ innings, then came back the next day to beat the Yankees, 6-0, on a six-hitter.

He lost again to Johnson, 3-1, on July 22, but a significance in this game was when he struck out for Johnson's 3,000th career strikeout, the first in major-league history to reach that mark.[13]

He matched up against Johnson for the third time on August 9 and lost 2-1, giving up runs in the seventh and eighth innings after allowing no hits through 5⅔ innings.

On August 15, Covey lasted two innings, giving up four runs in an 8-6 loss to the Red Sox. In the August 16 *Plain Dealer*: "Stan Coveleskie seems to have reached the stage where he is either a mark for the opposing batsmen or unusually effective. There are no halfway stations in his skill. Yesterday he seemed to have less than usual."[14]

It was his last game of the season. On August 25, it was reported he was under the weather,[15] and four days later, he suffered from rheumatism[16] and returned home to Shamokin.

1924 SEASON

On January 1, 1924, Coveleski married his late wife Mary's younger sister, Frances, who had been caring for his two sons in Shamokin. His hometown newspaper, the *Shamokin News-Dispatch*, reported on February 1 in a story headlined "Shamokin's Popular Twirler of Cleveland Ball Team Married to Miss Frances Shivetts, Sister of His First Wife, Who Died in 1920" on page one, although the names of Mary and her father were incorrect:

> Stanley Coveleskie, premier pitcher of the Cleveland American league team and well known local citizen, started the new year in a commendable manner by taking onto himself a wife in the person of Miss Frances Shivetts, a respected young woman of this city.
>
> Although the marriage took place on New Year's day, news of the event has just been learned in this city. They were married in Uniontown (north of Shamokin), after which the famous ball player and his estimable wife returned to Shamokin, where they have gone to housekeeping on West Walnut street.

The bride is the charming daughter of Mr. and Mrs. Francis
Shivetts and is the sister of Stanley's first wife, nee Victoria
(according to her death certificate, her first name was Mary,
although other records list it as Mae, and her father's name was
Joseph, not Francis) Shivetts, who died in the spring of 1920. She
has been caring for Stanley's two children while the renowned
hurler was with the team on the road. The friendship that followed between the foster mother and the star pitcher culminated
in their marriage at the beginning of the year.

Coveleskie will leave for Hot Springs, Arkansas, February
10, where he will go into training with the other pitchers of the
Cleveland team. Although 'Covey' was unfortunate in being ill
during the latter part of last season, he held the record of allowing the least number of runs per game in which he pitched. He
is at present in the best of condition and feels certain that he
will even better last season's record. Cleveland, with the addition
of hard-hitting first baseman George Burns, should have a fine
chance of duplicating its feat of 1920 by winning the pennant the
coming season.[17]

While Covey gained a wife, he lost his catcher about a week later
when Steve O'Neill, the catcher for most of his career, was traded. Stan
often mentioned that they were in synch to the point that he didn't need
a sign for what pitch to throw. Like Covey, Steve came from the coal
region of Pennsylvania—Minooka, near Scranton.

"I'd be crazy to say I will not miss Steve," Stan said after the trade.
"When a fellow pitches to the same catcher for eight years, he gets to
understand his every move, and I suppose Steve feels the same about
me. Steve and I worked together so long I guess we went along just like
a machine."[18]

O'Neill was sent to Boston on January 7 with Bill Wambsgass, Dan
Boone, and Joe Connolly for first-baseman George Burns, catcher Allie
Walters, and infielder Chick Fewster. Steve batted .265 during his 13
seasons with Cleveland and .263 overall. He broke in with Cleveland
in 1911 and became the full-time starter in 1915. After the trade, he

played only four more years—one with Boston, one with New York, and two with St. Louis. The trade brought Burns back to Cleveland, where he had been a reserve in 1920 and a part-time starter in 1921. He won the American League MVP award in 1926 when he batted .358. He had a .307 average during a 16-year career.

Coveleski arrived at spring training apparently recovered from rheumatism and confident he could return to his old form.

"I never felt better or stronger in my life," he told Henry Edwards of *The Plain Dealer.* "I have been working my arm for two weeks, and it feels loose and strong. I have thrown a lot of spitters, and there was not the least soreness. I'll be all right."[19]

Earlier, he said one of his problems was that he had trouble sleeping on trains, which would take a toll on him toward the end of the season. Covey usually would start the opening game of each series and on the road that followed a train ride.[20] As he aged—he was 34 when the 1924 season began—the lack of rest seemed to have more of an impact on him.

Edwards also reported that Coveleski had trouble with his teeth the previous season and was under his normal weight. Whatever the reasons, Coveleski had been struggling, and he and the Indians hoped that would change.

Manager Tris Speaker planned to build his 1924 pitching staff around Covey and George Uhle, who went 26-16 in 1923 and led the league in victories, starts (44), complete games (30), and innings pitched (357⅔), although his ERA (3.77) was a full run higher than Covey's. At least there was optimism. Stan told Edwards at the end of spring training:

> I don't just think I am all right again. I know it. Since I had
> those teeth that were bothering me taken out, I have had no
> rheumatism. My arm never felt better. I am strong in every way.
> I have had no sore arm at all this spring. It has not hurt me to
> throw curve or spitter. I never was more able to stand hard work.
>
> I know I will be able to win more games than last year, for
> I will have a better hitting team behind me. The fact that I led
> all the league pitchers in effectiveness shows that I did not pitch
> such bad ball even though I did not win so many. It so happened,

though, that the other manager always picked his best pitcher to work against me, and our fellows did not get the runs behind me. But that is baseball.

But, this year, they will regard Uhle as the Cleveland pitcher they have to beat, and possibly I will not draw as strong opposition as last year. I am not kicking, though. I am willing to pitch against any of them, and if Speaker wants to start each series with me as he formerly did, I will be ready.

I have read Speaker intended to switch and not start each series with me for the reason I am a poor sleeper on a Pullman and possibly not as well fitted to go out and pitch as I would be if I had a good night's rest. There is something in that, all right, but when a fellow is in as good condition as I am, he ought not to notice it much. But, it is up to Spoke.[21]

Coveleski didn't start the season opener, and things didn't improve. He was 1-4 during the first two months of the season, and there were reports that he may be sent to the bullpen. He seemed to turn things around in June, when he went 6-2, including five straight wins. Two were in relief, and two were complete games, 2-1 over the Yankees and 4-1 over the White Sox.

He was inconsistent the rest of the year, going 3-3 in July, 4-4 in August, and 1-3 in September. He did have several strong outings, beating the eventual World Series champion Nationals, 2-1, on July 28, the Red Sox, 1-0, on six hits on August 5, the Nationals, 5-1, on August 13, and the Yankees, 1-0, on five hits on August 27. But he also had several of his worst outings. On July 6 at Chicago, he was pulled after two-thirds of an inning when he gave up four runs on a walk and four hits. On July 23, he failed to get an out in a start at Boston and was charged with four runs on a walk and three hits.

Not only did he have his second straight losing season, but his ERA shot up to 4.04, his worst year to date. Despite his struggles, he continued to be a workhorse. In his final 13 games, all starts, after the July 23 game at Boston, he pitched 11 complete games, including two shutouts, and averaged more than eight innings per start. He went 6-7 in those games, partly because of a lack of run support from the Indians, who scored three or fewer runs in seven of those games.

The Indians also faded, finishing in sixth place with a 67-86 record and 24 1/2 games behind the eventual world champion Washington Nationals. Uhle slipped to 9-15 with a 4.77 ERA. The lone bright spot was 24-year-old Joe Shaute, from Peckville, northeast of Scranton, who went 20-17 with a 3.75 ERA.

In his final game on September 22, he lost to the New York Yankees, 10-4, giving up 13 hits and seven earned runs in a complete game. Five of the Yankees' runs came in the top of the ninth inning, and three were unearned because of a throwing error by catcher Luke Sewell, Joe's younger brother. He held Babe Ruth to a single in four at-bats.

That also was his final game for the Cleveland Indians. On December 11, Coveleski was traded to defending World Series champion Washington for pitcher Byron Speece and outfielder Carr Smith.

"I regret to part with Covey," Speaker said, "but it was a case of trying to help Covey as well as ourselves. For two years, Stanley has not been of much value to us because of his health. The fact that he has been at his best during the hot weather makes me believe that the change to Washington climatic conditions cannot help but be a benefit to him. Again, we know that Covey had come to be a pitcher who put the ball over the plate and let the batters take their swing, with the result, they were putting dents in our short right-field wall and screen. The fences are further away in Washington, and the outfielders can go and get drives that would be doubles in Cleveland."[22]

Covey finished his nine years in Cleveland with a 172-123 record, a 2.80 ERA, 193 complete games, 31 shutouts, and 856 strikeouts. Speece pitched in 30 games during the next two years for Cleveland, going 3-5. He finished his four-year major-league career with a 5-6 record and a 4.73 ERA in 62 games. Smith didn't play at all for Cleveland.

"I slipped a little bit over there," Coveleski said in a 1974 audio interview with Eugene Murdock. "They had to make a change. I had a good year, (then) the next year, I started out, and the first thing you know, my arm dropped. It didn't hurt me or nothing. I'd go pitch about two, three innings, and it still dropped. Didn't know what the hext it was. Everybody thought I am done see. I went to see Bonesetter Reese in Youngstown, and he said there's nothing the matter with your arm. Well then they left me go. I went to a dentist, and I had bad teeth see, and he said, Covey, that poison's in your system for a long time. He said if you get your teeth out, your arm will come back. But that's what it was, all this moisture from your teeth."[23]

Even though he had a lot of success in Cleveland, he wasn't sad to leave and believed his attitude there might have affected his performance in the last two years.

"I never did like Cleveland," he said later. "Don't know why. Didn't like the town. Now the people are all right, but I just didn't like the town. You know I got to a point where I wouldn't hustle no more. See, a player gets to be with a club too long. Gets lazy, you know."[24]

He joined an older staff in Washington led by Walter "Big Train" Johnson, one of the all-time greats of the game. When Covey joined the Nationals, he was 35, and Johnson was 37.

"The pitching staff is not worrying me now, at least for 1925, even if we do have the oldest aggregation of hurlers ever assembled on one club," Washington manager Bucky Harris said after the trade. "I think Coveleskie will give us two good seasons. I am proud of that deal, for I think Covey will be able to step right in and win for us."[25]

If people thought Covey was finished, they were in for a surprise.

"I plan on giving him plenty of rest between games," Harris wrote in an article previewing the season. "With rest, a warmer climate, which always helps a veteran pitcher, and a championship club behind him, I'll be surprised if Coveleskie doesn't win fifteen or twenty games."[26]

1925 SEASON

At the start of spring training, Speaker lectured his young pitching staff in Cleveland about the importance of not tipping batters on which pitch they would throw. He said that may have been another thing that contributed to Covey's recent struggles:

> Going back to Addie Joss and continuing down to today, such
> pitchers as Walter Johnson, Shocker, Ed Walsh, Dutch Leonard,

and Stanley Coveleskie have tipped their hands to the batters now
and then. One reason why Covey failed to remain so successful
was that batters, if they were watchful, could tell whether Stan
was going to throw a spitter or just bluff one.[27]

Whether it was a warmer climate, more rest between starts, not having to start a series after not being able to sleep on a train, or becoming
aware that he may have been tipping his pitches, Covey certainly turned
things around in 1925.

On April 16, in his first start for the Nationals, he went six innings,
gave up 10 hits and three earned runs against the Yankees, and left trailing, 5-0. But Washington rallied and won, 7-5, with five runs in the top
of the ninth against reliever Urban Shocker on three consecutive hits—a
two-run double by Sam Rice, a two-run homer by Goose Goslin, and a
solo shot by Joe Judge.

In his next game, nine days later, Covey got his first win, 8-7, over
the Yankees. Through six innings, he allowed four hits and had an 8-1
lead but then allowed three runs in the seventh and was charged with two
runs in the eighth before being relieved.

He did not lose again for almost three months, running his winning
streak to 13. In 17 starts, including four no-decisions, he pitched ten
complete games, including two shutouts, and allowed more than three
earned runs in only two of those starts.

His best stretch during the streak was from June 20 to July 8, when
he pitched five straight complete games, including two shutouts, defeating Cleveland, 2-1; New York, 1-0; Philadelphia, 4-1; Boston, 11-0; and
Chicago, 10-2.

The 2-1 win over Cleveland on June 20 was the first over his former
team. He had gone seven innings in a no-decision at Cleveland on May
19, giving up three runs in seven innings before Washington rallied for a
4-3 win. In his first win against the Indians, he allowed six hits and one
run, struck out five, and walked two. George Burns drove in the only run
for Cleveland with a single in the top of the sixth. Washington scored in
the bottom of the inning on a groundout when the Indians failed to turn
a double-play.

He shut out the Yankees, 1-0, on four hits on June 25, striking out five and walking two. Catcher Muddy Ruel drove in the only run with a single in the second inning. In the 4-1 win over the Athletics on June 29, he allowed only a ninth-inning run on a double by Jimmy Dykes and a single by Bill Lamar, which ended Covey's 20-inning scoreless streak. He blanked the Red Sox on four hits on July 3, then allowed only two seventh-inning runs against the White Sox on July 8. Between the run he allowed to Cleveland and the two to Chicago, he allowed only one run during a stretch of 36 innings.

In five games against his former team, he was 4-0, all complete games, with one no-decision. He allowed eight earned runs in 42 innings for a 1.71 ERA, gave up 41 hits, struck out 12, and walked seven.

He won his 14th game (13th straight) on July 26 in New York. He trailed 4-3 after eight innings but got the win when the Nationals scored four in the top of the ninth and held on for a 7-4 victory.

Covey stumbled briefly, and his win streak ended. He lasted only three innings, giving up nine hits and five runs in an 11-1 loss to the White Sox on July 30. Then he lasted five innings in losses to Detroit, 3-2, on August 3, and St. Louis, 3-0, on August 7. He recovered and went 6-1 with two no-decisions the rest of the season. His only loss in that stretch was August 21 at Detroit, 1-0, when he gave up a run in the bottom of the 11th inning on a sacrifice fly by Lu Blue.

On September 7, Labor Day, Washington played a doubleheader in Philadelphia on what was labeled "Coveleskie Day" by his hometown. More than 500 fans traveled from Shamokin to Philadelphia's Shibe Park on a special train to pay tribute to their baseball hero. Judge Albert Lloyd was chairman of the Coveleskie Day committee. Stan's brothers Harry and John were among those who traveled to the game.[28] Coveleski was given several gifts from his hometown fans, including a silver set.

Walter Johnson pitched the Nationals to a 2-1 win in the first game. Covey was not as successful in the second game. He gave up eight hits, five runs, and walked four in 6⅓ innings. Washington led 5-0 before he allowed four runs on four hits in the bottom of the fifth and another run on a walk, and two hits in the seventh. The Nationals came back to win the game, 7-6, with two runs in the eighth.

Coveleski ended the season by shutting out Detroit, 1-0, on five hits in the second game of a doubleheader called because of darkness after six innings on September 17, then on September 22, defeated Cleveland, 3-2, for his 20th win of the season.

That was Covey's final start of the regular season because two days later, Washington swept a doubleheader from Cleveland to clinch its second straight American League championship.[29] Stan Coveleski was heading to his second World Series.

Washington had ended June with a 45-23 record but trailed Philadelphia in the standings until June 30. The teams battled for the league lead until August 19, when the Nationals moved into first place to stay. They ended the season 96-55, eight games ahead of second-place Philadelphia.

Coveleski finished the year with a 20-5 record, the top winning percentage in the league at .800. He also led the league with a 2.84 ERA in 241 innings. He completed 15 of 32 starts, including three shutouts. Even manager Bucky Harris, who had predicted Covey would win 15 or 20 games, had to be a little surprised at the showing by his new pitcher. Walter Johnson, who injured his leg sliding into first base on September 17 and only pitched seven innings during the last two weeks of the regular season, went 20-7 with a 3.07 ERA, and Dutch Ruether was 18-7 and 3.87.

The offense was led by outfielders Sam Rice, who batted .350, and Goose Goslin, who batted .334 and hit 18 home runs

Before the World Series started, temperatures dropped, which didn't help the soreness in Coveleski's shoulders.

"Covey is receiving special attention from Trainer Martin on the rubbing table," wrote John B. Keller of the *Evening Star*. "Mike works on the shoulder and back muscles of the old-timer every morning, then with adhesive tape straps, Covey's back so tightly after the task is completed that the pitcher holds himself as stiffly as a horse under a checkrein. Covey is not 'kicking' about the treatment, though, and figures he will be in fine fettle as soon as the weather moderates."[30]

Game One
Washington 4, Pittsburgh 1
October 7, Forbes Field

When the Nationals arrived in Pittsburgh, manager Bucky Harris announced that Johnson and Coveleski would pitch the first two games in the best-of-seven series. Johnson seemed to be recovered from what was called a charley horse that had sidelined him for almost two weeks.[31] He limited the Pirates to five hits and a single run on a homer by Pie Traynor leading off the bottom of the fifth inning, struck out 10, and walked one.

Washington took a 1-0 lead in the second on a home run by right-fielder Joe Harris, scored two more in the fifth on a bases-loaded single by center-fielder Sam Rice with two outs, and added an insurance run in the top of the ninth on a two-out single by third baseman Ossie Bluege.

Game Two
Pittsburgh 3, Washington 2
October 8, Forbes Field

Before the second game, there was a report that Covey was "suffering with several varieties of lumbago."[32] But for seven innings, Covey reminded people of his World Series performance of 1920. He limited the Pirates to four hits and one run through seven innings. The run scored on a two-out homer by shortstop Glenn Wright in the fourth inning that tied the score after first-baseman Joe Judge had given the Nationals a 1-0 lead with a leadoff homer in the second.

After an error by shortstop Roger Peckinpaugh—his first of two in the eighth inning—allowed second-baseman Eddie Moore to reach base, Covey gave up a two-run homer to right fielder Kiki Cuyler for a 3-1 Pirates lead.

The Nationals threatened in the fifth when Peckinpaugh and Buddy Ruel led off with singles, and Coveleski reached base on a fielder's choice sacrifice bunt to the pitcher that loaded the bases. But Sam Rice and Bucky Harris hit grounders for force-outs at home, and Goose Goslin grounded to first to end the inning.

In the top of the ninth, Washington again loaded the bases with no outs against pitcher Vic Aldridge on a single and two walks. A run scored on pinch-hitter Bobby Veach's sacrifice fly to deep center, but Dutch Ruether, who batted .333 in 108 at-bats during the regular season, struck out as a pinch-hitter for Coveleski, and Rice grounded out to end the game.

Coveleski allowed seven hits and two earned runs in eight innings. He struck out three and walked one, but the two home-run pitches proved to be the difference.

"We lost a tough ball game today," manager Bucky Harris said. "Every chance we had slipped away from us, and we had many chances, I admit. Maybe we were too confident behind the good pitching of Coveleskie; maybe we were too eager and, as a consequence, too nervous."[33]

Covey was reminded of another game from the 1920 regular season. The Nationals lost Bluege in the sixth inning when he was knocked unconscious by a pitch from Pittsburgh's Aldridge. Ossie Bluege recovered but missed the next two games.

Game Three
Washington 4, Pittsburgh 3
October 10, Griffith Stadium
The Series shifted to Washington, and manager Bucky Harris decided to start Alex Ferguson rather than left-hander Dutch Ruether because the Pirates hit better against lefties. In fact, Ruether didn't pitch at all in the Series. Ferguson pitched seven innings and held the Pirates to six hits and two earned runs. He trailed after six innings, 3-1, but the Nationals scored one in the sixth inning on a leadoff homer by Goose Goslin and two in the seventh on a sacrifice fly by Joe Judge and an RBI single by Joe Harris for a 4-3 lead. Firpo Marberry pitched two scoreless innings in relief to save the win for Washington.

Game Four
Washington 4, Pittsburgh 0
October 11, Griffith Stadium
Washington, leading the Series, 2-1, now had its sights set on clinching the championship at home with Walter Johnson and Coveleski scheduled to pitch the next two games. The Nationals were even more confident when Johnson, who pitched through another charley horse in the third inning,[34] limited the Pirates to six hits in a 4-0 shutout that gave them a 3-1 lead in the Series. He struck out two and walked two. The Pirates' only threat was in the second inning when they had runners

100

on second and third with two outs before Johnson got out of it with a groundball to second.

Washington scored all its runs in the third inning on back-to-back homers—a three-run line drive by Goose Goslin and a solo shot by Joe Harris.

Game Five
Pittsburgh 6, Washington 3
October 12, Griffith Stadium

Covey started Game Five looking to clinch his second World Series title, but he struggled from the start.

With one out in the first, Max Carey and Kiki Cuyler hit back-to-back singles. After a liner to left for the second out, Covey walked Pie Traynor to load the bases, but the threat ended on a grounder to the mound. The Nationals gave him a 1-0 lead in the bottom of the first on an RBI double by Goose Goslin, scoring Sam Rice, who had opened with a single and moved to second on a sacrifice bunt by Bucky Harris.

Pittsburgh took a 2-1 lead in the top of the third inning. Coveleski walked two with one out, then gave up an RBI single to Clyde Barnhart and a sacrifice fly to Traynor. In the fourth, the Pirates had runners on first and third on singles by Earl Smith and Eddie Moore, but Covey got out of it with a grounder to first.

Washington tied the score with a leadoff homer by Joe Harris in the bottom of the fourth and had Pirates pitcher Vic Aldridge in trouble when Buddy Ruel singled and Ossie Bluege, who returned to the lineup after the beaning in Game Two, doubled to put runners on second and third with one out. But Covey struck out on four pitches without swinging his bat, and Sam Rice grounded out to first for the final out. With Covey struggling, manager Bucky Harris was second-guessed for not pinch-hitting for him.[35]

Coveleski settled down in the next two innings, retiring the 3–4–5 batters in order in the fifth and throwing only five pitches in the sixth, ending the inning with a 1–6–3 double-play grounder after a throwing error by shortstop Roger Peckinpaugh, one of eight he committed in the Series, had put a runner on first.

Covey was done in the seventh inning. After getting Aldridge on a grounder to third, he walked Eddie Moore, then gave up consecutive singles to Carey, Cuyler, and Clyde Barnhart, the last two driving in runs for a 4-2 Pittsburgh lead. He lasted 6⅓ innings, allowing nine hits, four walks, and four runs. He threw 122 pitches, including 36 in the third inning, and three of the four batters he walked scored.

Washington made it 4-3 in the bottom of the seventh when Sam Rice's single drove in Nemo Leibold, who led off with a double, but winning pitcher Aldridge put the Nationals down in order in the eighth and ninth innings, and Pittsburgh added single runs in the last two innings.

Game Six
Pittsburgh 3, Washington 2
October 13, Forbes Field

Washington took a 2-0 lead with single runs in the first two innings against Ray Kremer. Goose Goslin homered with two outs in the first, and Roger Peckinpaugh doubled home a run in the second. Pittsburgh tied the score in the bottom of the third on a groundout by Clyde Barnhart and a single by Pie Traynor. Eddie Moore scored the deciding run when he homered to lead off the fifth against Alex Ferguson. The Nationals didn't threaten again until the eighth when they stranded a runner at third. In the ninth, they couldn't drive home Joe Harris, who had doubled with one out.

Game Seven
Pittsburgh 9, Washington 7
October 15, Forbes Field

The deciding seventh game was pushed back a day because of rain. Washington again took an early lead with four runs in the top of the first against Vic Aldridge but again couldn't hold it. Aldridge faced eight batters but got only one out. He allowed two singles and three walks and was hurt by two wild pitches and two errors.

Walter Johnson started for Washington, seeking his third win of the Series, but as Covey had in Game Four, he struggled, especially in the later innings. After threatening in the first two innings, Pittsburgh broke through with three runs in the third on four hits. Washington extended its lead to 6-3 on a two-run double by Joe Harris in the top of the fourth, but Pittsburgh came back with a run in the fifth on consecutive doubles by Max Carey and Kiki Cuyler and tied the score with two in the seventh on a double by Carey and a triple by Pie Traynor.

Roger Peckinpaugh put the Nationals back in front, 7-6, with a solo homer in the eighth, but the Pirates got to Johnson for three runs in the bottom of the inning on doubles by Earl Smith, Carson Bigbee, and Cuyler. Pittsburgh's Ray Kremer pitched four innings for the win, and Red Oldham put Washington down in order in the ninth to save the 9-7 victory and give the championship to the Pirates.

Johnson, who gave up 15 hits and five earned runs, walked one and struck out three in the full eight innings. He threw 133 pitches, including 33 in the eighth. Manager Bucky Harris again was criticized for staying with his pitcher too long, just as he had done with Coveleski in Game Five.[36]

After the Series, Coveleski returned with the team to Washington, got his car, and drove home to Shamokin.[37] In five games in two World Series, he was 3-2 with a 1.74 ERA and four complete games. In 41⅓ innings, he allowed 31 hits, struck out 11, and walked seven.

Johnson pitched two more seasons for Washington before retiring. In 21 years with the Nationals, he was 417-279 with an ERA of 2.17. He pitched 531 complete games, including 110 shutouts, and struck out 3,509 in 5,914⅓ innings. In 1936, he was elected to the first class of the National Baseball Hall of Fame, along with Ty Cobb, Christy Mathewson, Babe Ruth, and Honus Wagner.

1926 SEASON

When the 1926 season started, nine spitball pitchers remained in baseball—Coveleski, Burleigh Grimes, Red Faber, Jack Quinn, Dutch Leonard, Urban Shocker, Allen Sothoron, Clarence Mitchell, and Allen Russell.

Covey and a few other teammates began their spring workouts in February at Hot Springs, Arkansas, before reporting to Tampa on March 1. Washington again had an older pitching staff that included Walter Johnson, 38; Coveleski, 36; Bullet Joe Bush, 33, who was acquired in a trade with St. Louis in February; and Dutch Ruether, 32. Manager Bucky Harris predicted the Nationals would repeat as American League champions if they won 96 games and got 21 wins from Johnson and Bush, 17 from Coveleski, 16 from Alex Ferguson, and 12 from Curly Ogden. He didn't mention Ruether, who had not signed a contract at that point.[38]

The season didn't go as Harris hoped. Covey came the closest to the prediction by Harris with a 14-11 record and a 3.12 ERA. He pitched 245⅓ innings and 11 complete games. But Johnson went 15-16 and Bush 1-8 before he was sold to Pittsburgh on July 1 when the Nationals were 13 games out of first. Ferguson was 3-4 in just 19 games and was traded to Buffalo of the International League on June 24. Ogden was 4-4 in 22 games before being optioned to Birmingham of the Southern Association in July. Ruether was 12-6 when he was traded to the Yankees on August 27.

Johnson gave Washington early hope when he beat Philadelphia, 1-0, on six hits in 15 innings in the season opener, and the next day Coveleski allowed only an unearned run and six hits in a 3-1 win. Even though the Nationals were competitive for most of the season and briefly were in first place in May, they spent most of the year at least ten games out of first. They finished the season 81-69, 15 wins short of Harris' goal, and in fourth place.

Covey's record was around .500 most of the season, but he did provide reminders of his younger days. He pitched two four-hit shutouts—10-0 against Boston on May 5 and 1-0 in 10 innings against Chicago on August 26. Five days later, he shut out Boston, 2-0, on five hits. He finished the season strong, winning five of his last six decisions, including a stretch of 23 straight scoreless innings. He allowed two or fewer earned runs in 20 of his 34 starts.

When the season ended, Covey returned to Shamokin to spend the next few months hunting in the mountains of Pennsylvania.

1927 SEASON

On February 4, Covey signed a contract to return to the Nationals, who looked to rebuild their pitching staff around him and Johnson. Covey immediately left for Hot Springs, Arkansas, to begin conditioning work before reporting to Tampa for spring training on February 28.

"Nobody on our club is worrying about Walter Johnson or Coveleskie, who are the only real veterans," manager Bucky Harris said early in spring training. "They will be there."[39]

Harris hoped Curly Ogden would add pitching depth, but he showed up overweight,[40] had a terrible spring, and was sent to Buffalo in the International League. He never made it back to the majors, finishing his five-year career 18-19.

The pitching staff Harris had envisioned never came together. Walter Johnson broke his ankle on March 10 when he was hit by a line drive. He didn't return until May 30 and never regained his old form. He went 5-6 with a 5.10 ERA in his final season in baseball.

Joining the Nationals was Coveleski's old friend and former manager Tris Speaker. He resigned as Cleveland's manager after the 1926 season when there were accusations that he and Ty Cobb of the Detroit Tigers had wagered on games and conspired to throw games in 1919 to allow the Tigers to finish in third place and qualify for a share of the World Series money. Both players were cleared, but they were declared free agents. Cobb signed with Philadelphia, where he batted .357 in 1927 and .323 in 1928, then retired at age 41 with a .366 lifetime average in 24 seasons. Speaker spent the one year in Washington, where he batted .327, then joined Cobb in Philadelphia for his final season, when he batted .267. He finished his 22-year career at age 40 with a .345 lifetime average.

When spring training started, Covey worked harder than he had for several years, determined to prove he wasn't finished as a pitcher.[41]

With Johnson injured, Coveleski started the season opener against Boston, even though he was suffering from nerve trouble in his right leg.[42] He pitched well for three innings but struggled in the fourth and asked to be taken out, despite giving up just four hits and one run. He left with a 6-1 lead, and Washington won, 6-2.

Arm trouble kept Covey out for the next ten days. He returned April 22 and lasted six innings at Boston, allowing one run on two hits before tiring. He didn't pitch again until May 2 and lasted only two innings against New York, giving up five hits and four runs (two earned) in the

Nationals' 9-6 loss. The next day, he tried to pitch in relief but struggled again. He walked the first batter he faced, Babe Ruth, to load the bases, then gave up an RBI single to Lou Gehrig and walked Bob Meusel to force in another run before striking out Tony Lazzeri to end the inning. New York won, 6-4.

On May 8, he started at St. Louis but left after two innings because of a sore arm. He allowed one run, one hit, and two walks.

In the *Evening Star* on May 10, John B. Keller wrote: "The nature of Covey's trouble is being kept a deep dark secret by those in direct charge of the club. One time he has a sore hip; another time, he withdraws from a game voluntarily because he has developed a kink in his salary wing; still another time, the weather was not quite right for the veteran spit-baller, and finally, it is said, he has a sore elbow. At any rate, it is admitted that something is wrong with the old-timer."[43]

The teeth issue also returned. In late May, he expected to return to the mound after having a piece of a tooth removed from his jaw.[44] But his problems were more than an abscessed tooth. His arm pain contin-ued, and he left the club to see muscle specialist Bonesetter Reese in Youngstown, Ohio.[45]

Coveleski's days with Washington were over. On June 17, he was given his unconditional release by the Nationals. According to a later report by the *Shamokin News-Dispatch*, Stan's hometown newspaper, Bucky Harris didn't want to release Covey. Harris wanted Coveleski to rest for a month and return when his arm was stronger, but Covey asked for his outright release.[46]

He returned to Shamokin and said he would rest and attempt a comeback, even though many people believed his career was over.

In a June 19, 1927, editorial, *The Plain Dealer* wrote: "It is no disgrace for a baseball player to be knocked out by the master of the years. It is the inevitable climax. A Clarkson, a Young, a Plank, a Bender, a Johnson may seem destined to go on and on forever, but there is always an end. Happy is the ball player who, like Coveleskie, takes the count when the memory of his greatest achievements is still fresh and vivid.

"Of all the ball players who have endeared themselves to Cleveland enthusiasts, Coveleskie was one of the most modest and unostentatious.

He never played to the grandstand, and the plaudits of the grandstand never swelled his head. Neither did the razzing of hostile bleachers ever get his goat. He was a man with abundant nerve but without 'nerves.' A remarkable and admirable ball player was Covey, and it is indeed a sorrow to use the harsh word 'was.'"[47]

Washington finished the season 85-69, 19 games back of the American League and World Series champion Yankees, who were led by Ruth (.356 average and 60 home runs) and Gehrig (.373 and 47) and considered among the greatest teams of all time,

Ironically, Covey was in uniform with the Yankees when they were in Cleveland for a series in July,[48] but he didn't pitch for New York during the season.

On July 9, the *Shamokin News-Dispatch*, Coveleski's hometown newspaper, reported he had signed with the Yankees on July 7:

> The deal was consummated during the early hours of Thursday morning when Paul Kritchell, scout for the New York team, arrived in this city from Bridgeport, Conn., hot on the trail of Stanley to affix his signature to a Yankee contract. However, Stanley was at his fishing camp in the northern section of the state, and when Kritchell came here and was unable to get in communication with the heaver, he left with Harry Coveleskie, the Giant Killer, for the camp by automobile.
>
> Stanley was aroused from his slumbers and went in deep conference with Kritchell. When the little talk had been completed, the Shamokin pitcher had promised that he would be willing to talk terms with the Yankee management, and if satisfactory terms could be reached, he would be willing to join the Huggins club.
>
> Accordingly, the party left for Williamsport, where Miller Huggins, manager of the New York club, and Colonel Jacob Ruppert, owner of the team, were reached on long-distance telephone, and the terms were settled over the wire. It took only a few minutes to come to a definite understanding, and Stanley was mighty pleased with the agreement reached."

When Stanley left Washington, he nursed his arm and back carefully and told Kritchell that either (stet) have caused him any trouble, whatever, and he should be able to pitch just as he did a few years ago when he was the leading hurler of the American league.

Harry Coveleskie stated today that his brother is due to arrive home some time today and will leave immediately for the west as the Yankees are now making a swing through the other end of the loop."[49]

However, Covey's arm soreness persisted, and he couldn't pitch for the Yankees during the 1927 season.[50]

1928 SEASON

Even though Coveleski didn't pitch again in 1927, Yankees manager Miller Huggins must have believed Covey still had some strength in his right arm because on December 21, 1927, he signed Covey to a contract for the 1928 season.

At the end of January, before heading to Hot Springs to prepare for spring training with the Yankees, Stan told his hometown newspaper in Shamokin that his arm was healed and the problems were caused by several bad teeth, which he had extracted.

"Feels fine now," he said as he stretched out his right arm. "I feel that there is still plenty of it."

He was sitting with his brothers Harry and John and talked about how he had spent time getting into shape.

"I've been hiking about on the hills and mountains every day with the dog," he said. "Hunted hard the past fall and fished just as hard last summer.

"I'll say I like to hunt and fish better than anything else I do. This fall I spent two weeks hunting birds in Potter county and talk about sport. I've got a setter up there, and it's a dandy dog for birds. Got quite a few grouse at that.

"As for fishing, found one of the best trout streams in Potter county last spring. Two miles from the nearest road and full of trout up to a foot and fourteen inches. That is true sport."[51]

As much as he loved his time alone in the woods, hunting and fishing, he wasn't ready to abandon throwing a baseball in front of tens of thousands of screaming fans. So, he gave it one more try.

For a while, it seemed Covey's arm had recovered enough to help the Yankees, who were coming off back-to-back American League championships. In his first game, he pitched two hitless innings in relief against Washington on May 2. In his first start on May 6, he survived a shaky start to beat Chicago, 4-2. The White Sox loaded the bases with no outs in the first on two singles and a walk, but he got out of it with a line-drive double play by Lou Gehrig at first base and a grounder to second baseman Tony Lazzeri. Covey went 6⅓ innings, allowed seven hits and two walks, and struck out two. He was supported by Gehrig's two-run homer in the first and Joe Dugan's solo shot in the second.

He struggled in his next start on May 12, giving up six hits and five runs in two innings against Detroit. He allowed five singles and four runs in the second and was pulled after a leadoff triple in the third by Harry Heilmann. The Yankees came back to win the game, 8-7, with a run in the bottom of the ninth.

Covey's next two starts were his best of the season, both complete-game victories. He beat St. Louis, 4-3, on six hits on May 17, and Boston, 14-4, on eight hits on May 22. But his days of starting and finishing games were over. His longest outing the rest of the way was seven innings on June 30, when he gave up four runs against Boston, a 7-6 win that raised his record to 5-0. He pitched 10⅓ innings the rest of the season, including just 1⅓ on July 9 against St, Louis, when he gave up five runs and seven hits in a 12-6 loss, the final decision in his career.

Stan's final major-league game was on August 3 at St. Louis. He pitched 1⅔ innings in relief with the Yankees trailing 4-0. He allowed four hits and four runs, but only one earned. He was pulled in the seventh after giving up a two-out, two-run triple to Lu Blue and an RBI single to Frank O'Rourke, the last batter he faced in the majors.

Coveleski finished the year 5-1 with a 5.74 ERA. He pitched 58 innings, gave up 72 hits and 20 walks, and struck out five. The Yankees swept St. Louis for their second straight World Series title. Covey received a half share of the World Series money that the Yankees players earned.[52]

The 1928 Yankees set a major-league record with nine members of the team who eventually would be elected to the Hall of Fame: Earle Combs, Lou Gehrig, Tony Lazzeri, Babe Ruth, Leo Durocher, Waite Hoyt, Herb Pennock, Stan Coveleski, and manager Miller Huggins. A tenth future Hall of Famer was Bill Dickey, who made his major-league debut with the team on August 15, 12 days after Covey's final game. Durocher was elected to the Hall based on his career as a manager.

On May 24, 1928, the Yankees defeated the Philadelphia Athletics, 9-7, in a game that had 13 future Hall of Famers in the lineup: Combs, Ruth, Gehrig, Lazzeri, Durocher, and Hoyt for the Yankees; Ty Cobb, Tris Speaker, Mickey Cochrane, Lefty Grove, Eddie Collins, Al Simmons, and Jimmie Foxx for the A's, who were managed by future Hall of Famer Connie Mack. Tom Connolly was also part of the game and was elected to the Hall as an umpire.

Coveleski, who was 39 when he retired, pitched in the major leagues for 14 seasons and compiled a 215-142 record, a .602 winning percentage. He had a 2.89 earned run average and led the league in 1923 (2.76) and 1925 (2.84). In 450 games, he pitched 3,082 innings, 38 shutouts, and 223 complete games. He struck out 981 and walked 802.

Stan Coveleski during training at Hot Springs in the 1920s. (Photo is from the Steve Steinberg collection and used with permission.)

Stan Coveleski climbing on rocks during training at Hot Springs in
the 1920s. (Photo is from the Steve Steinberg collection and used with
permission.)

Stan Coveleski takes a break during training at Hot Springs in the 1920s. (Photo is from the Steve Steinberg collection and used with permission.)

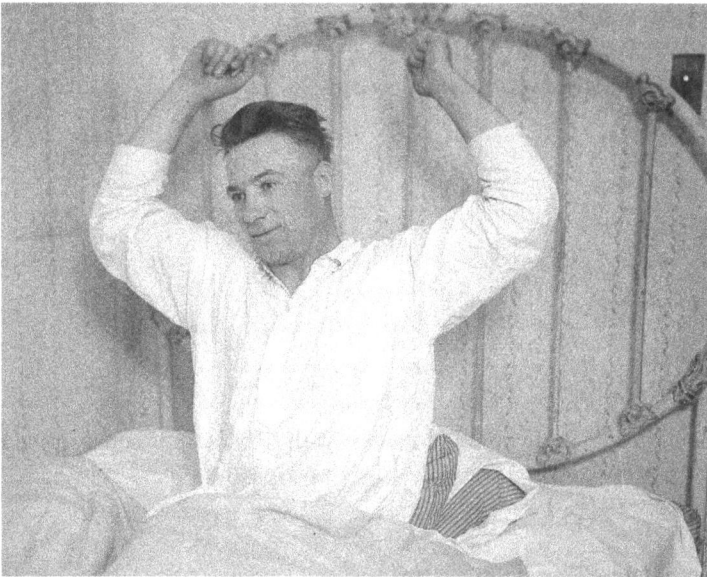

Photo from Stan Coveleski's personal album. (Photo is from the Steve Steinberg collection and used with permission.)

Stan Coveleski during the 1924 season with Cleveland. (Photo is from the Steve Steinberg collection and used with permission.)

Above: Stan Coveleski at breakfast in 1924. (Photo is from the Steve Steinberg collection and used with permission.)

Left: Stan Coveleski with Washington Nationals. (Photo is from the Ernie Harwell Sports Collection, Detroit Public Library, and used with permission.)

Stan Coveleski was honored by his hometown on September 7, 1925, when 500 people traveled on a special train from Shamokin to Philadelphia, where Covey pitched the second game of a doubleheader for the Washington Nationals against the Philadelphia Athletics. With Covey are members of the "Shamokin Day" committee. From left are John Coveleskie (brother), B. Lee Morgan, Harry Coveleski (brother), Ollie Bramhall, J.C. MacElwee, Stan Coveleski, Albert Lloyd, and Con Graeber. (Photo is courtesy of Larry Deklinski.)

Covey spits into the glove of catcher Muddy Ruel when they were teammates with Washington. (Photo is from the Steve Steinberg collection and used with permission.)

Stan Coveleski in 1925 when he played for Washington. (Photo is from the Steve Steinberg collection and used with permission.)

Stan Coveleski, left, and Slim Harriss of the Red Sox when they faced off in the 1927 season opener. (Photo is from the Steve Steinberg collection and used with permission.)

Stan Coveleski pitching for the Yankees in 1928. (Photo is from the Steve Steinberg collection and used with permission.)

Stan Coveleski, center, with Yankees teammates catcher Benny Bengough and pitcher Waite Hoyt, probably during spring training in 1928. (Photo is from the Steve Steinberg collection and used with permission.)

8

Life after baseball

Twenty years after Stanislaus Anthony Kowalewski walked away from the coal mines of Shamokin for an uncertain future in baseball, Stan Coveleski walked away from the major leagues for an uncertain future out of baseball. Three things he knew: His post-baseball life would include hunting, fishing, and chewing tobacco.

After his release from the Yankees, Covey returned to Shamokin, where he owned a house at 821 West Walnut Street. In April 1929, soon after his father died unexpectedly on March 19,[1] he accepted a job to coach and pitch for an independent team in South Bend, Indiana, the home of the University of Notre Dame, Studebaker Corporation, and Bendix Corporation. He had no connection to South Bend, but he had a job offer that didn't involve returning to the coal mines.

"I was managing the amateur ball club," he said years later. "They paid me a pretty good salary, and I stayed here."[2]

His wife and sons moved to South Bend in 1930 and lived at 1038 W. Napier Street. Around that time, he opened the Stanley Coveleski Service Station at 1012 Western Avenue. The 1930 census still showed him living on Walnut Street in Shamokin and proprietor of a service station.

"We moved from Pennsylvania," his wife, Frances, said. "We had a nice place (there). But he got to playing ball out here. Then we ran across this place, and some Polish people had it, and we didn't do much to it. We kept it the way it was."[3]

Stan played ball for several years and shared his baseball knowledge and stories with young men in the community, including during a 10-week lecture series sponsored by the local Falcons organization, a private Polish club established in South Bend in 1894. That was a change for a man who had little to say during his major-league career.[4]

Covey didn't have the service station for too many years because gasoline was in short supply when the Great Depression began around 1929, and businesses struggled to survive. Afterward, he would get up in the early morning hours, put in a chew, collect some minnows from a small pond in his backyard, and head to his favorite fishing spots.

People in Shamokin hoped their baseball hero would settle in his hometown, and Covey occasionally would tell people that he would return to Shamokin someday. He did return, but those trips weren't a permanent move. He went back to hunt in the mountains around Potter County, visit family members, and attend funerals in Shamokin.

On August 18, 1937, the *Shamokin News-Dispatch* spoke to Stan's brother, Harry, to clarify reports in other newspapers that Stan had moved to Schuylkill Haven, south of Shamokin, in 1935 and was working as a "motor salesman" there:

"Harry, who recently opened a café here and named it the 'Giant Killer,' says Stanley still is a resident of South Bend, Ind., where he has been living since he dropped out of the major-league spotlight. The former Cleveland, Washington, and New York Yankees' moundsman is a proprietor of a successful gas station located along the Lincoln Highway on the outskirts of South Bend. Harry declares there is a 'Stanley Coveleskie' residing in Schuylkill Haven, but that it is not his brother who won fame by pitching Cleveland to the World Series championship in 1920."

One of Stan's return trips to Shamokin was another sad time in his life—the funeral for his younger son, Jack, who died on July 17, 1938, at age 18. The cause of death was aortic dilation of the heart, with a contributing cause of rheumatic endocarditis, which likely resulted from rheumatic fever in the days before penicillin was in widespread use.

There was a short notice in the *Shamokin News-Dispatch* on July 20:

> The funeral of Jack Coveleskie, son of Mr. and Mrs. Stanley
> Coveleskie, South Bend, Ind., formerly of Shamokin, who died
> over the weekend at the home of his parents, will be held at 9:00
> tomorrow morning from St. Stanislaus Church. Burial will be in
> the parish cemetery. The body is resting at the home of Mr. and
> Mrs. Joseph Mrowka, 31 South Shamokin Street, prior to the
> funeral.[5]

Mrs. Mrowka was Frances' sister Susan.

Occasionally, Covey would attend baseball games and take part in old-timers games. One of those was on July 3, 1938, at League Park, when members of the 1920 Indians team, led by Tris Speaker, played an exhibition against members of the 1908 Cleveland Naps and 71-year-old Cy Young. The 1920 team won 8-0. Covey's spitball still had some movement when he threw to catcher Steve O'Neill.[6] He also attended the tribute to Babe Ruth at Yankee Stadium on April 27, 1947.

When Covey wasn't fishing, he worked in his garden or watched television, including baseball games. Some days he looked back at his glory days in baseball by paging through the scrapbook he had made, or he autographed photographs or baseballs for fans who still remembered him.

"I liked to give autographs," he told Rod Roberts in 1981. "I don't think I ever refused one."[7]

On March 27, 1945, Covey suffered a heart attack and initially was listed in critical condition,[8] but he bounced back as he did with every setback during his baseball career.

Covey returned to Shamokin in 1964 for the city's centennial celebration, when he was honored as a "distinguished son of Shamokin" in one of the parades and at a banquet.[9] He was inducted into the Cleveland Baseball Hall of Fame on August 7, 1966, along with outfielder Larry Doby and catcher Jim Hegan.

His greatest honor came in 1969 when he was elected to the National Baseball Hall of Fame in a unanimous vote by the Veterans Committee of the Baseball Writers Association of America. The call came on February

3 from Ford Frick, the baseball commissioner from 1951 to 1965 and a founder of the Hall of Fame in 1939, but Covey was out fishing. His wife, Frances, answered the telephone.

"Mr. Ford Frick called here, and Covey was fishing," she recalled during the interview with Rod Roberts in 1981. "He said, 'I'd like to speak to Mr. Coveleski.' I said, 'He's gone fishing.' He said, 'I suppose you're his wife.' He said he wanted to be the first to congratulate him. He was elected into the Hall of Fame. I couldn't talk for a second, and when I came to myself, I said, 'Well, I think it's about time.'"[10]

It was a conversation she and Frick laughed about later.

"It makes me feel just swell," Coveleski said when asked how he felt about his selection.[11]

"I figured I'd get it sooner or later, but I wasn't sure I would live long enough," Covey told Tom Kutza in 1969.

Joining Coveleski in the Hall of Fame class of 1969 were two other Pennsylvania natives, Stan Musial from Donora (south of Pittsburgh) and Roy Campanella from Philadelphia, and Waite Hoyt, another unanimous selection by the veterans' committee.

The induction took place on July 28 in Cooperstown, New York, but his hometown held a special testimonial for him several weeks before then. On July 3, a banquet was attended by 500 people at the Pleasant Hill Lodge in Ranshaw, not much more than a stone's throw from where Covey was born, and a parade was held in his honor as part of Shamokin's Anthracite Days celebration.

When he entered the hall for the testimonial, he was cheered for several minutes and received five standing ovations during the program. Among the gifts he received was a $1,000 check from area residents. Coveleski family members gave him a plaque carved out of a 20-pound piece of Anthracite coal with a photo of him surrounded by photos of his four brothers, which he later donated to the Hall of Fame.

Before the testimonial, he autographed more than 400 balls, bats, and gloves. He signed testimonial programs for 45 minutes at the end of the event.[12]

Ten days later, Stan turned 80, two weeks before he and Frances drove to Cooperstown.

He began his Hall of Fame speech, saying, "I'm no speaker. I'm a coal miner." At one point, he choked up and almost couldn't finish. He talked about working in the mines as a boy and how he learned to pitch by throwing rocks at tin cans. He ended abruptly, saying, "I think that's about all I have to say."[13]

"They had a great time for him," Frances told Rod Roberts in 1981. "Covey's a good listener. He's not much of a talker."[14]

In his acceptance speech, Musial paid tribute to Covey: "When I think of Stanley Coveleski, I think of my father. He was a Polish immigrant from Poland, and he was a great baseball fan. And when I was young, I always remember him talking about Babe Ruth. I know how thrilled he would be here today, not only with me but also with Stan Coveleski."[15]

Covey's plaque at the Hall of Fame summarizes his career, although his total victories are incorrectly listed as 214 instead of 215, and his ERA is listed at 2.88 instead of 2.89:

STANLEY ANTHONY COVELESKI
Philadelphia A.L.   1912
Cleveland A.L.   1916–1924
Washington A.L. 1925–1927
New York A.L.   1928
Star pitcher with a record of 214 wins,
141 losses, average .603, E.R.A. 2.88.
Won 20 or more games in 5 seasons. Won
13 straight games in 1925. Pitched and
won 3 games for Cleveland in 1920
World Series with E.R.A 0.67.

Cassidy Lent, manager of Reference Services for the National Baseball Hall of Fame and Museum, explained the discrepancy: "The statistics written on our plaques are believed to be accurate at the time they were cast. However, as more research is done and errors are found in the records, many of our older plaques are now not accurate. It is very difficult to change them, so we make it known in the Plaque Gallery that some of our plaques are not factual, but most likely were at the time they were made."

Several days after the induction ceremony, Stan returned home to South Bend and was admitted to St. Joseph Hospital in fair condition with possible pneumonia.[16]

One of the last great tributes for Covey while he was living, was in 1976, when he was elected to the Polish-American Sports Hall of Fame on June 11 in Detroit. On July 25, 1977, he attended the first Old-Timers Game at Wrigley Field in Chicago. Gary Stein of the *Rockford Morning Star*, Illinois, wrote in a column: "Stan Coveleski, an 88-year-old legend, was there. His hands are so brittle he can hardly sign autographs, but he gave it his best shot."[17]

Stan and Frances returned to Cooperstown for the Hall of Fame ceremony every year for the next decade, often stopping in Shamokin to visit family and friends before or after the trip. Their last trip to Cooperstown was in 1979 when Stan was 90.

As his health declined, he stopped traveling. He also gave up fishing.

"I got a dizzy spell while fishing and fell back," he told Rod Roberts in 1981. "I came home and gave the car keys to my son and quit (driving and) fishing. Nobody told me. I did it myself.[18]

But he never gave up chewing tobacco.

"I chewed tobacco every day since I was a kid," he said in 1981. "If my doctor told me today to quit chewing, I'd quit. I put a chew in this morning, and I won't take it out till noon."[19]

Stan Coveleski died on March 20, 1984, at 93, in a nursing home in South Bend after a lengthy illness. Services were held on March 22 at St. Stephen's Catholic Church, and he was buried in St. Joseph Cemetery.[20] He was the oldest living Hall of Famer at the time.

The day after Stan's death, Bill Moor, sports editor of the *South Bend Tribune*, recalled Covey in a column: "Covey lived a robust life almost to the end. Even when he had a heart attack while fishing out in his boat several years ago, he shrugged it off as hunger pains, rowed to shore, and went to a bar where he had a limburger cheese sandwich and a couple of bottles of beer. 'The next day, I had to walk down to the doctor's,' Covey recalled. 'He put me in a hospital for a while.'"[21]

After his death, Covey received two more honors.

South Bend opened the newly constructed Stanley Coveleski Regional Stadium at 501 West South Street in 1987, bringing minor-league baseball back to the city. The stadium became known as The Cove. The first team, the South Bend White Sox, was an affiliate of the Chicago White Sox. The team's name was changed to the South Bend Silver Hawks in recognition of the Studebaker Silver Hawk, manufactured near the stadium. In 1996, the team became part of the Arizona Diamondbacks minor-league system.

In 2013, owner Andrew T. Berlin, who had bought the team in 2011 and made extensive improvements to the stadium, sold the naming rights for the field to Four Winds Casino in South Bend, and the stadium became Four Winds Field at Stanley Coveleski Stadium. Part of the agreement included the erection of a six-foot bronze statue of Coveleski at the stadium. The statue was dedicated on August 6, 2016. The team became affiliated with the Chicago Cubs in 2014 and was renamed the South Bend Cubs.

In Covey's hometown of Shamokin, a granite monument made to look like Anthracite coal was dedicated on August 23, 1997, on Market Street. Ed Cove, son of Stan's brother John, was the guest speaker, and Shamokin radio personality Tom Kutza was the master of ceremonies at the program. Kutza instigated the idea for a memorial during a radio show in 1995.

"I used to have a talk show in that era," Kutza recalled. "Dick Kashner was one of the gentlemen there when I was doing a talk show about something else, and typical me, out of nowhere, I said, 'You know we have a baseball Hall of Famer in Shamokin, and nobody seems to know.' I said, 'Why don't we do something? Why wasn't something done about this guy?' And that's what started the whole thing. And Ron Bradley, who was was the mayor, and Dick Kashner looked at each other and said, 'Let's do something.' So, they started raising money, and that's how that monument happened, because of the talk show on WISL."[22]

The Shamokin Area Lions Club sponsored the project.

Underneath an image of Covey was a summary of his career, which follows the plaque at the Hall of Fame and lists incorrect numbers for his career wins and ERA:

STANLEY A. COVELESKI
Born July 13, 1989, in Shamokin, PA
Died March 20, 1984
Inducted into the Baseball Hall of Fame 1969
Philadelphia A.L.   1912
Cleveland A.L.   1916–1924
Washington A.L.   1925–1927
New York A.L.   1928
Star pitcher with a record of 214 wins
141 losses, average .603, E.R.A 2.88
Won 20 or more games in 5 seasons. Won
13 straight games in 1925. Pitched and
won 3 games for Cleveland in 1920
World Series with E.R.A. 0.67
Sponsored by
Shamokin Area Lions Club

Ed Cove, who died in 2013, was among Covey's closest living relatives at the time.

Stan's son William died in 1985, and his wife Frances died in 1992 in South Bend.

Above: Present-day house at 1038 West Napier Street in South Bend where Covey lived after he retired from Major League baseball. (Photo by Harry J. Deitz Jr.)

Left: Present-day house at 821 West Walnut Street where Covey lived in Shamokin before his family moved to South Bend, Indiana, in 1930. (Photo by Harry J. Deitz Jr.)

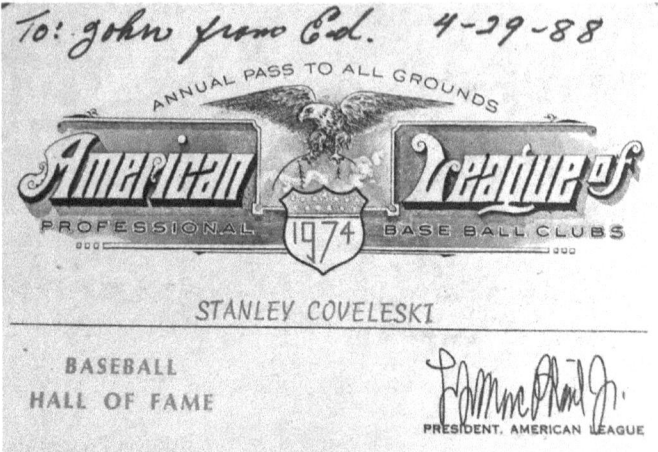

To: John from Ed. 4-29-88

ANNUAL PASS TO ALL GROUNDS

American League of

PROFESSIONAL 1974 BASE BALL CLUBS

STANLEY COVELESKI

BASEBALL
HALL OF FAME

PRESIDENT, AMERICAN LEAGUE

Lifetime pass allowing Stan Coveleski to attend American League games. The card later was given by Stan's wife, Frances, to his nephew Ed Cove in 1988, then passed to Ed's brother John Coveleskie. (From the collection of Rosalie Coveleski Moyer.)

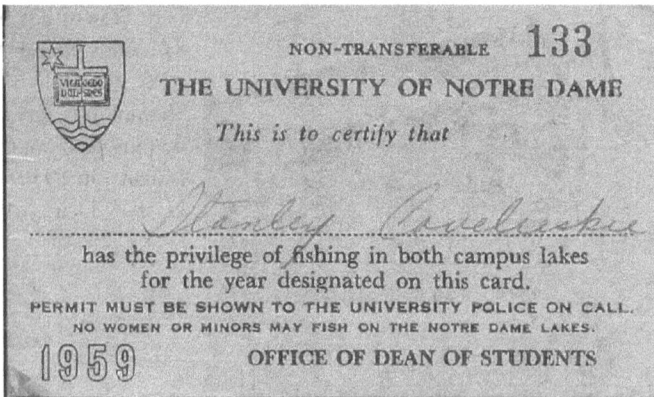

NON-TRANSFERABLE 133

THE UNIVERSITY OF NOTRE DAME

This is to certify that

Stanley Coveleskie

has the privilege of fishing in both campus lakes for the year designated on this card.

PERMIT MUST BE SHOWN TO THE UNIVERSITY POLICE ON CALL.
NO WOMEN OR MINORS MAY FISH ON THE NOTRE DAME LAKES.

1959 OFFICE OF DEAN OF STUDENTS

Fishing card that allowed Stan Coveleski to fish the campus lakes at the University of Notre Dame, South Bend, Indiana. (From the collection of Jarad Zarkowski.)

Stan Coveleski, left, with Steve O'Neill and Tris Speaker on July 3, 1938, when their 1920 Indians team played members of the 1908 Cleveland Naps in an old-timers game. (Photo is from the Steve Steinberg collection and used with permission.)

Autographed photo of Stan Coveleski, probably in his 80s. (Courtesy of
Rosalie Coveleski Moyer.)

Baseball autographed by Stan Coveleski. (Courtesy of Bruce Victoriano.)

TESTIMONIAL

In Honor of

STANLEY COVELESKIE

On Entry to

BASEBALL HALL OF FAME

THURSDAY, JULY 3rd, 1969

Pleasant Hill Lodge—Ranshaw, Pa.

Cover of the booklet for the Shamokin testimonial for Coveleski in 1969. (From the collection of Bruce Victoriano.)

STANLEY COVELESKIE

Baseball

Hall of Fame, 1969

STANLEY COVELESKIE

The twin communities of Shamokin and Coal Township honor with pride our native son—Stanley Coveleskie—upon his election to the Baseball Hall of Fame.

Born in Luke Fidler, Coal Township on July 13, 1889, Stan learned the fundamentals of the national pastime on local sandlots—particularly on Bunker Hill.

Helping in Stan's development was the fact that he came from Shamokin's greatest baseball family. The Hall of Fame pitcher had four brothers who made their own marks in the baseball world. Jake, who later gave his life in the Spanish-American War, played a fast brand of local ball and his brother, Frank, starred in the high minors. The other two Coveleskie boys made the majors. John played considerable ball for the Philadelphia A's and the St. Louis Browns and Harry became famous as the "Giant Killer," a pitcher for the Philadephia Phillies.

Stan graduated from the Shamokin team of the Atlantic League to the Lancaster and Atlantic City teams of the Tri-State League where a four-year record of 73 wins and 51 losses earned him a shot at the Philadelphia A's in 1912. After winning 2 out of 3 there, Stan went to Spokane, Washington and Portland, Oregon for the next three seasons where he had big seasons. The local righthander then came back to the Majors for 13 seasons until retirement in 1928.

Stan joined the Cleveland Indians in 1916 and proceeded to rack up a 32-29 record the following two seasons. Then, in 1919, Stan started on a streak of four straight 20 plus victory seasons. Perhaps the highlight of his career came in the 1920 World Series against the Brooklyn Dodgers when Stan became the first pitcher in modern baseball to win three games in one World Series. In doing this, Stan gave up only two runs and 15 hits while striking out 8 and walking only two.

(Continued on page three)

JAKE
COVELESKIE

FRANK
COVELESKIE

JOHN
COVELESKIE

HARRY
COVELESKIE

A page from the booklet for the Shamokin testimonial for Coveleski in 1969. (From the collection of Bruce Victoriano.)

THE WHITE HOUSE

WASHINGTON

June 16, 1969

Dear Stan:

The President has requested me to convey his greetings and
congratulations to you on the occasion of your election to the
Baseball Hall of Fame. This is one of the highest honors
that can come to an athlete, and I am pleased to join your
friends and fans in Shamokin and Coal Township in this tribute
to you.

Best wishes for many more pleasant and productive years.

Sincerely,

Captain James A. Lovell, USN
Consultant to the President for
Physical Fitness and Sports
NASA Astronaut

Mr. Stanley A. Coveleskie
c/o Mr. B. Lee Morgan
City Hall
Shamokin, Pennsylvania 17872

A page from the booklet for the Shamokin testimonial for Coveleski in 1969. (From
the collection of Bruce Victoriano.)

Tribute from One

Who Knew Him

FORD C. FRICK

A man's talent hardly could be more natural than Coveleskie's, as a teenager he warmed up for professional ball by pitching four or five amateur games, and he was ready. And, because it was his own way of doing things, this youth from the coal mines fell into an admirable habit immediately, that is of perfection in his job. To Coveleskie his job was to win twenty games, so that is what he did.

The lad from Shamokin and Coaltown started winning twenty ball games per season when he was 19 years old, with Lancaster in the Tri State League, in 1909. His record was 23-11. Stanley went on to win twenty at Atlantic City and at Spokane, so when he arrived at Cleveland he was a well known figure in the baseball trade, as a wholesale winner. With the Indians, enforced by a thorough education in four minor leagues, Coveleskie won nineteen games in 1917 and then ran off four straight twenty-game campaigns. Traded to Washington he promptly dashed off a 20-5 season as a Senator.

In the 1920 World Series he pitched the first, fourth and seventh games, won them all, over the full route. It was typical of him, when he is assigned to something he goes through with it, regarding it a responsibility. He pitched more shut-outs than anybody in 1917 and 1923 and won thirteen in a row in 1925. That is a spread of nine seasons of reliability. Before settling in the majors he pitched sixty-four games at Portland, Ore., most by any pitcher in the Pacific Coast League. The year before he led another league in strike-outs. In eight of his seasons Coveleskie worked 290 or more innings.

I knew Covey personally in my baseball writing days, am pleased to join with the people in his home countryside in honoring this gentleman whose career in turn, honors them. Like the name of a notorious killer struck subdued respect in a western cow town, Coveleskie was respected and widely known around the baseball circuit as a bead eyed stalwart, who when he went out to get you, was in the habit of completing the job. There must be something in the stock of Shamokin and Coal Township to produce a citizen with the qualities of Covey.

S/   FORD C. FRICK

Commissioner of Baseball

1951 - 1965

A page from the booklet for the Shamokin testimonial for Coveleski in 1969. (From the collection of Bruce Victoriano.)

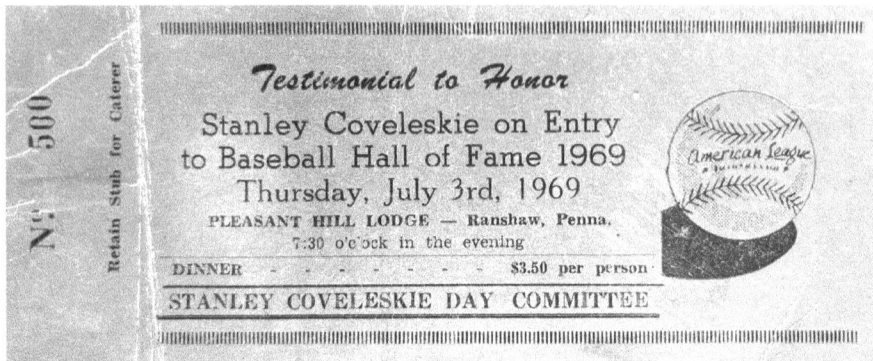

Ticket for the 1969 Shamokin testimonial for Stan Coveleski. (From the collection of Tom Kutza.)

Stan Coveleski with unidentified young and old fans when he returned to Shamokin in 1969 for a testimonial. (From the collection of Tom Kutza.)

COVELESKIE HONORED—Stan Coveleskie, a Shamokin native, who was named to the Baseball Hall of Fame, was honored during the Anthracite Days celebration in Shamokin early in July. Coveleskie is shown, with his wife, waving to admirers during a parade in his honor. Seated is B. Lee Morgan, who served as chairman of the Coveleskie Testimonial Committee.

Frances and Stan Coveleski during parade in his honor in July 1969. With them is B. Lee Morgan, chairman of the Coveleski Testimonial Committee. (Courtesy of *The News-Item*, Shamokin, July 6, 1969.)

Coveleski burial plot in St. Joseph Cemetery, South Bend, Indiana. (Photo by Harry J. Deitz Jr.)

The statue of Stan Coveleski at Stanley Coveleski Regional Stadium, South Bend, Indiana. (Photos by Harry J. Deitz Jr.)

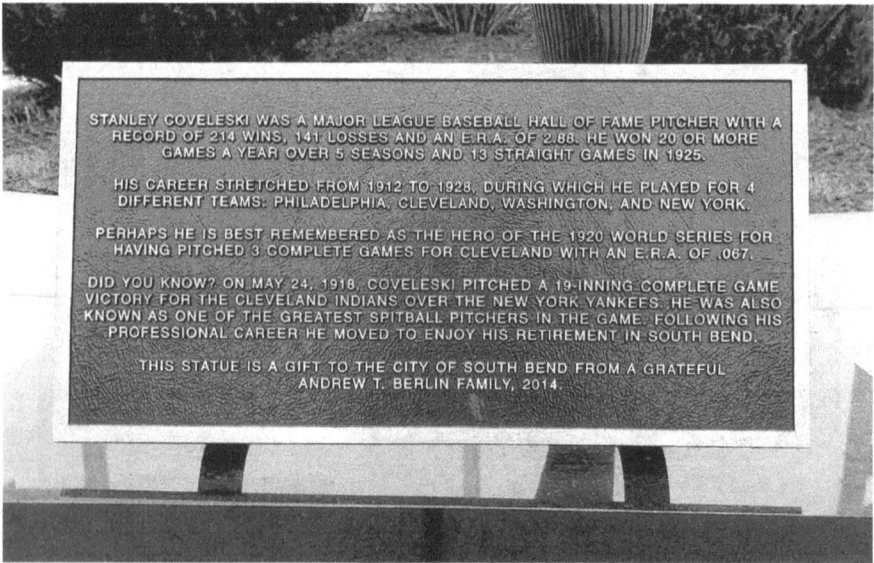

The plague at the base of of Stan Coveleski's statue at Stanley Coveleski Regional Stadium, South Bend, Indiana. (Photos by Harry J. Deitz Jr.)

The Coveleski monument on Market Street, Shamokin. (Photo by Harry J. Deitz Jr.)

Coveleski monument unveiled

■ *Project initiated in July of 1995 by friends and members of the Shamokin Lions Club.*

By Mark Gilger
Staff Writer

SHAMOKIN — A nice crowd turned out Saturday afternoon to honor Hall of Fame pitcher Stanley Coveleski, whose monument was unveiled during dedication ceremonies at a grassy plot on Market Street across from Independence Fire Company.

Ed Cove, nephew of Shamokin native Stanley Coveleski, served as guest speaker. Cove, who resides in Berwick, talked about several experiences he enjoyed with his famous uncle. He commended everyone who made the monument project a success and said he was glad to see various youth baseball players in attendance at the ceremonies. Cove extended special appreciation to members of the Stanley Coveleski Monument Project including project co-chairmen Ronald "Lum" Bradley and Dick Kashner and committee members Bernie Romanoski Sr., Robert Probert and Dr. Robert Coutts.

Project committee members distributed commemorative autographed baseball cards of Coveleski and displayed various old-time photos of Coveleski's major league career.

Tom Kutza, popular longtime radio broadcaster for WISL Radio, served as master of ceremonies. Kutza recalled his interviews with Coveleski and mixed in his usual humorous anecdotes. Kutza talked about how the Stanley Coveleski Memorial Project started in July 1995. He praised everyone who donated money to the project and all the volunteers who helped raise funds.

Bradley also offered remarks and thanked everyone who assisted in making the memorial project very successful.

The project was sponsored by Shamokin Area Lions Club and the monument was erected by Peter Molesevich of Kulpmont.

Coveleski was a star pitcher in the major leagues for 14 years. He played with Philadelphia, Cleveland, Washington and New York in the American League and compiled a career mark of 214-141. His career earned run average was 2.88 and he won 20 or more games in five seasons. He won 13 straight games in 1925 while pitching for Washington and won three games in the 1920 World Series while hurling for Cleveland. The Indians went on to win that

Newspaper clipping showing Ed Cove, Stan Coveleski's nephew, at the dedication of the monument in Shamokin on August 23, 1997. (Courtesy of *The News-Item*, Shamokin, August 25, 1997.)

9

Remembering the man

Stan Coveleski was known by many names other than variations of his birth name. He was called the Silent Pole because he rarely spoke, and the Big Pole, even though he was 5-foot-11 and 166 pounds. He was labeled the Ice Box and Brother Stan because he was cool and calm. But he was best known by the name he preferred and called himself—Covey.

There was so much more to him than the names.

Coveleski was a teammate of 18 Hall of Famers: Home Run Baker, Charles Bender, Eddie Collins, Herb Pennock, and Eddie Plank with Philadelphia; Tris Speaker and Joe Sewell with Cleveland; Goose Goslin, Bucky Harris, Walter Johnson, Sam Rice, and Speaker with Washington; and Earle Combs, Leo Durocher, Lou Gehrig, Waite Hoyt, Tony Lazzeri, Herb Pennock, Babe Ruth with New York. And he competed against dozens of others elected to the Hall of Fame, including Ty Cobb, Rogers Hornsby, George Sisler, and Harry Heilmann, and some who weren't, including Shoeless Joe Jackson.

He played for four Hall of Fame managers—Connie Mack, Tris Speaker, Bucky Harris, and Miller Huggins.

INTERVIEWS AND COMMENTARY

Those who had the honor of interviewing Coveleski cherished their time with him, especially in the later years of Covey's life. They worked hard to get comments from the man who remained the "Silent Pole" all his life, but he occasionally became motivated to talk. Eugene Murdock,

Lawrence Ritter, and Rod Roberts were among the lucky ones who recorded interviews with Covey long after his playing days. So was Tom Kutza, a well-known radio personality in Covey's hometown of Shamokin, who interviewed Coveleski when he came into town to be honored before his Hall of Fame induction in 1969.

The sportswriters who covered him in the 1920s struggled to get comments from Coveleski, but they also had a lot of respect for how he played the game.

The writing styles in newspapers in the 1920s were much different than what is shared 100 years later but no less interesting. Although many of the terms and phrases have changed, those old-time newsmen succeeded in capturing the essence of Covey.

Tom Kutza's interview
He never forgot where he came from.

Tom Kutza, a well-known radio announcer for WISL in Shamokin, clearly remembers his June 30, 1969, interview with Covey, the audio recording of which he found several years ago:

"The fact that he was so proud to be a coal cracker. This is the stuff that I love to talk about.

"I met him—I'll never forget—it was a very hot summer day. He had a long-sleeve white shirt on with the sleeves rolled up. I shook his hand. I was thrown into it in a hurry because our sports director went on vacation, and all of a sudden, it was put a suit on, go down there and interview Stanley Coveleski.

"I get in there, and I introduce myself, and he shook my hand. He was a little old guy, thin, wrinkled, the whole thing, and he had a handshake—his hands, his paws were huge. He had a grasp.

"He had an Acme bag filled with F&S Beer (which was brewed in Shamokin). He said, 'Do you want a beer?' I said, 'Thank you, but I'm working.' He said, 'That's the best damn beer I ever had.'

"He sat down, and he opened up like everything was yesterday. He talked about he never had a suit. I guess the owner of one of the clubs bought him a suit. He got on the train at the old Reading station on

Independence Street, and he said he was never away. He was very bashful. They did call him the Silent Pole.

"I winged it because I don't eat sports, but I found out what the guy was about, and that's what really mattered to me. He was such a gentleman. I can feel his presence as I speak. He said he ate hot dogs by himself because he was that bashful. He was getting thrown into a situation in life where there's a lot of people, and he's not coal mining anymore.

"What I'm really getting at is he was so genuine. Nowadays, these, may I call them clowns, they make so much money. These guys did it for the love of the game.

"It was him. He never forgot where he came from, believe me. He was just so gentle, so kind. He loved kids. He mentioned something to the kids about keep trying, don't give up, all that neat stuff. That's the gentleman that impressed my heart, impressed me so much, like it happened yesterday."[1]

Billy Evans article
A most unusual and likable character.

One of the most interesting and insightful articles about Covey's personality was written by umpire Billy Evans and published on February 23, 1921, in *The Plain Dealer*. Evans, who was inducted into the Hall of Fame in 1973, was an American League ump from 1906-1927 and was a sportswriter.

In his opinion piece headlined "'The Silent Man' in Which Billy Evans Tells Why You Hear Little of Coveleskie," he labeled Covey "one of the least understood men in baseball." He called Covey "a wonderful pitcher, a remarkable champion, yet he has been in the limelight but little . . . Not until the world series of 1920 . . . was the worth of Coveleskie really appreciated."

In the archived article, parts of which are faded and difficult to read, he described Covey as "the silent man" and wrote: "Coveleskie is the retiring type. He seldom speaks except when spoken to, and unless you noticed his name in the box score, you would scarcely know he was a pitcher of the Cleveland club."

Most interesting are the last few paragraphs of Evans' article:

"He will sit through a ball game munching a chew and never speak a word from a position of a remote corner of the bench. Perhaps no player on the club is more interested or pulling harder for victory, but it is not his style to be explosive. He can enthuse in silence.

"Every now and then on every ball club, some argument comes up. It shows interest to have such things happen, However, there is a certain point where it is best that all such arguments cease for the general good of the club. On the Cleveland bench, it is not uncommon to break up such discussion by having someone shout:

"'Shut up, Coveleskie. You are always starting trouble on the bench. If you would keep quiet, all would be well.'

"Such a remark usually gets a laugh, other players enter into the spirit, jump on Coveleskie, and the argument subsides and is forgotten. Meantime Coveleskie smiles, keeps on chewing but says nary a word.

"Never once has Coveleskie disputed the ruling of an umpire on balls and strikes. He accepts the bitter with the sweet. You could miss a half a dozen in a row on Coveleskie, and he would never say a word. He would keep working all the harder. In all my major league experience, Coveleskie is one of the most unusual and likable characters I have ever encountered."[2]

Stuart Bell column
President smiled on him.

Another interesting article describing Covey was written by Stuart M. Bell in *The Plain Dealer* on June 19, 1921, after the Indians visited President Warren G. Harding in the White House on June 13, following their World Series championship of the previous fall. It was headlined, "Josh Covey Nearly Any Time, But Look Out on Days He Toils" and "Indian Spitball Artist, Beloved Over Entire American Circuit, Has Whole Heart and Soul in Team, Owner, and Fans."

Bell wrote: "The other day, two great men met in Washington. One was Warren G. Harding, president of the greatest country on earth, and the other was Stanley Coveleskie, star pitcher of the Cleveland Indians, a pitcher who, shortly before Mr. Harding became president, won three games in the world series with Brooklyn and clinched the baseball championship of the world for Cleveland.

"There was a touch of the dramatic in the meeting between Coveleskie and Harding, the one slightly bashful and ill at ease; the other calm, assured of bearing, but pleased.

"One large firm hand of the president grasped the right hand of the famous spitballer, while the other went to the pitcher's shoulder. The president had a kind word for every member of the Indians, but the president is a fan, and he had read of Coveleskie.

"The face of the country's president broke into a cordial, friendly smile as he grasped the pitcher's hand.

"'So you are Coveleskie,' he said. 'I believe your friends call you Covey, do they not?'

"The serious, honest face of the great hurler relaxed into a smile, though his eyes found it hard to look into the friendly ones of the president. They weren't used to looking at presidents, though had the president had on a baseball uniform and held a bat, the eyes would have steadied, bored through him, maybe with just a trace of compassion for what was going to happen to him when he, Covey, threw his spitter.

"Covey was the last of the long line of ball players to file out of the executive offices of the White House, the last to line up before the battery of cameras that waited outside.

"That afternoon, Coveleskie was called upon to pitch the last three innings of the game between Washington and Cleveland, going to the box after Cleveland had obtained a commanding lead. He had pitched a full game Saturday, but Covey always is ready to hold the enemy when victory is in sight.

"The Nationals, who had driven one Cleveland hurler from the box and hit another hard, were helpless before Coveleskie.

"The Pole pitched as only he can pitch when he is right, and there was reason for Coveleskie to be right that day. Hadn't the president of his country grasped his hand and called him Covey?

"How many times must Coveleskie, down in the mines of Pennsylvania, where he worked when a boy, dreamed of the day when he might see a president. That day a president had smiled upon him as a friend and called him Covey.

"The inspiration of the handclasp must still have been with Coveleskie Wednesday when he hurled eleven grueling innings and beat the Athletics, 6 to 5. It was his third victory in five days. Twenty-three innings of work is nothing for Coveleskie when his team needs him.

"The fans of every city in the American league love Stanley Coveleskie, those of Cleveland, of course, most of all, but how many of them know the real Coveleskie? How many of them know of the love Coveleskie has in his work, of the earnestness of his efforts, of the heartbreak he often suffers but shows to no one?

"Few fans know that on the morning of the day he is going to pitch, Coveleskie awakens with the thought of the work in hand uppermost in his mind.

"In the words of baseball players, he 'tightens up.'

"There is no smile on the face of Coveleskie as he sits at breakfast, at luncheon, or around the hotel lobby. His teammates who know him best simply nod to him. Those who haven't been teammates of Coveleskie long may stop and pass friendly greetings. These he returns, but quietly, almost gruffly.

"Those who know Coveleskie, not at all, may stop for a second and josh him. They only do it once. Strange as it may seem, Coveleskie, usually the most friendly and kindly of men, becomes suddenly antagonistic at a kidding remark and may give an answer that hurts.

"Even after the game, even though he wins, Coveleskie can not be joshed, hardly spoken to. You may tell him he made a wonderful hit, and he will smile, but tell him he made the opposing batters look like suckers, and he never even turns his head.

"But the next day, it is different. You can say anything to Coveleskie then, and he is ready to josh, talk about the game, or anything else.

"How many fans have ever seen Coveleskie smile in a ball game, winning or losing?

"When Coveleskie pitches, he pitches, and if you could pitch like Coveleskie, the president of your country would have an extra smile for you and would feel just a bit proud to shake the hand of a man whose first thought is for his team, the owner and the fans of Cleveland.[3]

Covey's SABR bio

He threw Joe Sewell into the lake.

Daniel R. Levitt wrote an article about Coveleski for the Society for American Baseball Research biography project. He shared a story about Covey's personality:

"Though he could be taciturn and ornery on days when he pitched, off the field, Coveleski was generally considered friendly, though not particularly talkative. Stan also indulged a lively but sometimes malicious sense of humor. At spring training in 1921 in Dallas, manager Tris Speaker invited the team down to his nearby home for a barbeque. Coveleski and shortstop Joe Sewell took a rowboat out on the lake. Once out a ways from shore, Covey asked Sewell if he could swim. The rookie replied in the negative, whereupon Coveleski shoved him into the lake and rowed away. A rescue party saved Sewell; Coveleski never explained himself, thinking the prank very funny."[4]

Roberts audio interview

He kept minnows in the bathtub.

During spring training, Covey liked to relax with his other favorite sport, fishing. He recalled that during an interview Rod Roberts conducted for the Hall of Fame in 1981:

"I used to go out fishing and throw the fish in my bathtub. A fellow went to take a bath and said how am I going to take a bath when my bathtub is full of minnows?"[5]

Carmichael column

A game without a spitter.

In a 1963 column, *Chicago Daily News* sports editor John P. Carmichael recalled this story about Coveleski throwing a spitter:

"One day during the pennant season, his catcher, the late Steve O'Neill, walked to the mound and begged: 'Don't make me stoop today or move around too much because I had a bad night. . . .'

"So Stan threw nothing but stomach-high fastballs inside and won his game . . . 'because the hitters thought I was setting 'em up for a spitter,' he explained."[6]

COMMENTS FROM PLAYERS

Joe Sewell
"He was one of the best spitball pitchers that I ever saw.

"Coveleski would throw that ball sidearm, and it would break like a curveball. I seen him throw that spitball when the wind was blowing against him. A right-hand hitter up there and he'd throw that ball sidearm, and I seen that right-hand hitter fall on the ground, and the ball would break over the plate. Strike. He was a great spitball pitcher, and he had great control.

"Speaker was our manager. When a club would come into town, normally you'd have a meeting, maybe the first day, maybe every day. On this particular day, Covey was going to pitch. Speaker said, 'How are you going to pitch to so and so, the leadoff man?' Covey says, 'I'm going to fire that spitter in there.' We'd discuss it. Speaker says, 'The second man, how are you going to pitch to him?' Covey says, 'I'm going to fire that spitter in there.' We got to about the fourth or fifth hitter, and Speaker says, 'Why Covey, you ain't going to throw nothing but a spitball ball today then?' Covey says, 'That's right.' And he opened up with a spitball and closed up with a spitball."

"He sure was nice. You take a lot of pitchers, and they rant and stomp and kick. You could make an error or a missed play behind Coveleski, and he'd never say a word. He was like Walter Johnson. He'd pat you on the back."[7]

Tris Speaker
Spoke, as he often was called, was the player-manager of the Indians when they won the 1920 World Series. After Covey won Game Four, Speaker said, "He not only is the best spitball pitcher in the country, but he also is one of the best pitchers in the land regardless of style of delivery."[8]

Glenn Myatt
In 1937 *Houston Chronicle* sportswriter Dick Freeman interviewed catcher Glenn Myatt, who played with Covey in Cleveland in 1923 and 1924:

"I asked Glenn who was the best pitcher he had caught in his many years behind the plate, and he didn't hesitate a second. 'Stan Coveleskie,' he said. 'That big Pole had one of the greatest spitters ever shown in the majors. It not only would break like a rifle shot, but he had perfect control of it. I've seen him come through with a spitball when it was three balls and no strikes if he figured there was a chance of the batter trying to lean against a fat one.'"[9]

Waite Hoyt

"He was a helluva good pitcher," said Yankee great Waite Hoyt, who was inducted into the Hall of Fame with Covey in 1969. "He never gave the hitter much above the knees. He was a real tough guy, too, and especially tough against the Yankees, as I remember."[10]

Lew Fonseca

Lew Fonseca played for Reds, Indians, and White Sox, 1921-1933.

"I was hitting .425 with the Reds one spring when we landed in Cleveland for an exhibition game, Coveleski was pitching, and he threw spitballs either overhand or sidearm. I fouled off about five and was telling myself, 'I'll get one of them,' when he suddenly let fly a fastball right over the plate. I never even moved a finger on the bat. Just went back and sat down."[11]

COVEY QUOTES

Coveleski didn't talk much, but what he did say was interesting. Here are some of his comments found in the Kutza interview and numerous articles, including the often-noted quote, "Baseball is a worrying thing."

"I was never a strikeout pitcher. Why should I throw eight or nine balls to get a man out when I got away with three or four?"

"They're all good pitches if you pitch them in the right spot at the right time. I used the spitball, but I didn't use it all the time. I had them looking for it. But if they're looking for a spitball and you throw something else, you'll have no trouble with them. You've got to mix them all up."

"I never did like Cleveland. Don't know why. Didn't like the town. Now, the people are all right, but I just didn't like the town."

"I never had no trouble with Cobb. I never had any trouble with good hitters. The ones that gave me trouble was bad hitters because I eased up on them. A good hitter I worked at."

"Every one of them fellows has a weakness. I've never seen a ball-player that didn't have a weakness. If you have control, you can pitch to the weakness and have no trouble at all."

"I had a lot of fun playing baseball. I enjoyed it. I'll tell you . . . you enjoy it as long as you can be up there winning . . . , but when you're not winning, it's a tough racket. You got four, five, six, or seven fellows looking for your job all the time. You worry all the time. There's always someone waiting to get in there. And if you're trying to get in and there's somebody else starting there, why you probably will never get in there. Baseball is a worrying thing."

ODDS AND ENDS

Covey's batting stats

Coveleski's batting skills didn't match what he did as a pitcher. He had a .159 lifetime regular-season batting average in the majors. In 1,197 plate appearances, he had 168 hits, including 26 doubles, 10 triples, one home run, and 81 RBIs. He walked 53 times and struck out 309. He was 1-for-15 in five World Series games.

Covey admitted he was not a good hitter, although he liked to hit against right-handers. He preferred not to run the bases so he could save his energy for pitching.

He had a .972 lifetime fielding average, committing 29 errors in 14 seasons.

Covey's advice to young ballplayers

"I don't care if you're an outfielder or an infielder; if you throw a ball, try to hit something. Pick an object out to hit it. There's no use throwing a ball if it don't mean anything to you. When you have to pick an object out, you're forcing your arm, and you're stretching your arm, and you'll get more speed.

"You got to keep at it all day. You can't just go at it once or twice a week. You got to go at it all the time. Never give up."[12]

Billy, the bat boy

Hal Lebovitz, the sports editor of *The Plain Dealer* in Cleveland, wrote a column in 1975, responding to a question about who was the bat boy for the Indians in 1920. He contacted some of the old players, including Coveleski.

"The first time we called, his wife said he was out fishing. The second time we caught him just as he was about to go to the nearest pond. The old spitball pitcher who won three of the Indians' five games in the '20 World Series, goes fishing every day the weather permits. 'I catch blue gills, bass, and pike,' enough for supper,' he says. He hasn't worked since 1929, when the Great Depression forced him to close his gas station. 'I got by,' he says. Probably on fish. Almost 85, he and his wife live in South Bend, and he says he'd rather go fishing now than watch baseball because 'sometimes I get too disgusted with the pitchers.' Sure, he knew who the batboy was. 'It was my son, Billy. And Doc Johnston's son, too. Both of them did it. I'm too old to remember for sure. But I know my kid was there.'"[13]

Successful brothers

Stan and brother Harry Coveleski combined for 296 wins and were among the best brother combinations in major-league history, although not close to Phil and Joe Niekro (539) and Gaylord and Jim Perry (529).

Rheumatism ads

Athletes endorsed products even during the early days of baseball. Covey's name was attached to newspaper advertisements for Mike Martin's Liniment, along with Walter Johnson, Ty Cobb, and George Sisler, during the time he played for Washington.

One of the ads had several headlines: "Coveleski Uses Magic Liniment, Keeps Free of Aches and Pains; Stiff, Lame, Rheumatic Folks Should Take Tip From This Great Pitcher; Knows How to Keep Spry, Free of Aches and Pains."

Covey was quoted in the ad: "I used Mike Martin's Liniment when I was with the Cleveland Club years ago, and a lot of the boys on that team still do. It's positively amazing what that liniment will do for aches, pains, sore arms, or stiffness."[14]

Mike Martin was a long-time trainer and then a scout for the Washington Nationals. There is no indication what compensation Covey and the others received for their endorsements.

Covey's name

Stanislaus Kowalewski wasn't the only one who changed his name during his baseball career. Connie Mack's given name was Cornelius Alexander McGillicuddy

Covey's top salaries

Stan's top salary was $10,000 in 1928 with the Yankees. He made $9,000 in his last year with Washington and $7,500 in his last year with Cleveland.[15]

All strikes

Covey claimed he once threw seven innings when every pitch was hit, missed, or called a strike.

Covey against the best

Covey said: "Babe Ruth and Ty Cobb were the best players I pitched against but don't forget Napoleon Lajoie and Home Run Baker—they

were some great ball players, too. But I wasn't afraid of any of them."[16]
Here are his stats against Ruth and Cobb, according to Retrosheet.org:

Covey's career vs.	Ruth	Cobb
At-bats	104	142
Hits	35	44
Doubles	10	9
Triples	1	2
Home runs	5	1
Walks	*48	11
Strikeouts	15	10
Batting average	.337	.310

* Includes 14 intentional walks

Hall of Fame votes

Covey was unanimously elected to the Hall of Fame by the Veterans Committee in 1969. Here are his vote totals by the Baseball Writers Association of America:

1 in 1938
2 in 1948
3 in 1949
1 in 1950
34 in 1958 12.8%

FAMILY MEMORIES

Stan had two children, William and Jack. William had one child, John Joseph, born and died on September 27, 1948. Jack died in 1938 at age 18. There are no direct descendants of Stan.

There are, however, many great-nieces and nephews—grandchildren and great-grandchildren of his brothers and sisters—some who met him when they were young and some who heard stories about him.

Here are some of their memories:

Rosalie Coveleski Moyer
Great niece of Stan, granddaughter of Stan's brother John

Uncle Stanley, when he would come to Shamokin when I was younger, would stay with us, or we would go see him wherever he was staying. This was when he was much older and no longer playing ball.

We maintained the Coveleski name. You may see an "e" at the end sometimes. My father would often sign his name with the "e" at the end.

Uncle Stanley had four brothers and three sisters. The one brother, Frank, had a very large family, maybe 10 children. He lived just outside of Shamokin. I remember going up there to that house at Fidler's Gap.

My great-grandfather (Anthony) lived with my dad for just a few years at 1536 West Arch Street, where I grew up.

The house (in Fidler's Gap) I remember going to, I remember us turning onto the street, and it was on the right-hand side. It had a really old-fashioned metal fence around it. It was a half a double. Aunt Elizabeth is who we would go see. I think she was one of Frank's daughters. I think she ended up acquiring the house. I was under 10. Sometimes we would take our dog. It was an older home. You go up two or three steps into the yard. A sidewalk went along the whole side of the house, and you often went in the back door. The kitchen was in the back, and there was a dining room and a living room as you came forward. Like three bedrooms upstairs and the yard kind of ran along to the side of the house. It was not a fancy house at all.

My dad was so proud of who he was and having been related to Uncle Stanley. He remembered being a little boy when his dad, my grandfather, was very active in getting a lot of people to go to Philadelphia (for the Stan Coveleski day in 1925). My grandfather was sort of the party coordinator to going down to a game in Philly. I guess they went down on a train.

Back in the day, they walked to the nearest colliery, and there was a big one in that area. My dad talked about that. About Stanley working at the colliery, like the pictures you see about the breaker boys sitting along stairsteps and sorting out the different sized pieces of coal. That was up along Route 61. It wasn't around the corner for them to walk, but it was probably less than two miles.

When he would come to the house and visit my dad and my mom, I was pretty small. We would sit on the front porch. He always wanted me to play softball. He always asked me if I was going to become a softball player. I remember sitting on his knee on the front porch and him talking to me and asking how is school going? And stay in school. And are you going to be a softball player Rosie? He would call me Rosie. He did speak very well, even though his parents spoke Polish. That was on the front porch on Arch Street. He would come in the summer and when he would do any traveling during the nicer weather months.

I always kind of thought that he had that drive in him to be something and to make something of himself. He just had that drive to make something of himself. Back in the day, everything was labor. You had a job, and you were a laborer of some sort, whether it was working in the colliery or you had to work with your hands. He had a drive to him. Some sort of a gumption.

He had a lot of loss in his life. That takes a toll on a person. I'm thankful he had a good relationship with Francie after Mary passed away and married her. I think he did the best he could under circumstances he grew up in. He found a skill that he was good at. He had a drive to him, an ambition, a motivation, and becoming a ballplayer.[17]

John E. Coveleski
Great nephew, grandson of Stan's brother John (Rosalie's brother)
When Stan used to come back in the offseason, he had a lot of people who knew him, and he'd spend time with his brother Harry. My grandpa had like a store, a billiard parlor in town. My dad told me stories about when he was a little boy, five or six years old, different guys would come into town that knew Harry and knew Stan, and they'd be sitting at the bar and having a beer and talking baseball. My dad had some great stories, and I tried to remember some from him.

I remember my dad and Uncle Ed going out when that field (in South Bend) was dedicated to him.

My wife and I went (to Shamokin) in '69 when he went in the Hall of Fame. And we were there at my parents' home, and Stan came out, and he's sitting there in the living room and thought I'd like to get a baseball signed by him. I jumped into the car and ran into Malett's sporting goods store in Shamokin. They didn't have a Rawlings or Spalding full-size baseball, so I got the closest I could get. It's almost like a junior league, but it's a baseball. He came out to the house, and he was sitting there in the living room and I went over and talked to him a little bit, and I asked him to sign it. He signed it "To John. Stanley Coveleski." I asked him a couple of questions about some of the ballplayers he played with.

I said, "Uncle Stan, how did you pitch to Ty Cobb?" He said: "You had to pitch inside to him because if you pitched outside, he could spray it to all fields. He had great bat control. You had to pitch inside and low to Cobb." I said, "How about Ruth? He said, "You pitched outside to Ruth." He said if you pitched inside, he'd pull it and kill you." I wish I could have spent more time with him.

When a guy like that hits town and they haven't seen him, and he was a major leaguer, everybody wants to spend time with him. If he went in town and there were guys that were 75 or 80 years old, they'd say, I'll take you out to dinner, or I'll buy you a drink. When he hit town, everybody wanted to spend some time with him.

I can't imagine sitting in the dugout with Lou Gehrig and Babe Ruth because he was with the Yankees in '28.

My dad told me he can remember going in town when Stan was with Washington, and he could remember his dad going down to the World Series in '25. He said he could remember standing there and seeing his dad get on the train. Him and Harry going down to the World Series to see that.[18]

Larry Cove

Great nephew of Stan, grandson of Stan's brother John. Larry's father, Ed, was the guest speaker at the dedication for the monument in Shamokin.

I met him when I was pretty young. He came to my father's home. When I met him, he was a pretty quiet fellow. He didn't say a lot.

I was at the induction in '69.

I remember the one story about throwing stones. He'd hang a can on a tree. I was really young. I might have been eight or nine when I met him.

(Rosalie's father, John, and Larry's father, Ed, were brothers and sons of John, who was Stan's brother. Ed shortened his name to Cove.)

The reason I know (for the name change) was my father employed 200 people in Berwick. He had a manufacturing company. That's one of the reasons why he shortened it, just to make it easier, as far as I know. They rebuilt railroad cars and built modular steel construction buildings. They built platforms for the army.[19]

Bill Covaleskie
Great nephew, grandson of Stan's brother Frank

I was just a teenager when I met him at the time of his induction at the Hall of Fame. They had a large testimonial dinner for him up in the Shamokin area, and I was up there with my father and lots of other family members.

A piece of Anthracite was chiseled and given to him with his picture in the middle and his four brothers, one of them being my grandfather, in the corners. He donated it to the Hall of Fame.

I spent a lot of time up there at my grandma's house when I was a kid. I spent probably a month every summer up there. It was in one of the small patches outside Shamokin, Sagon, which is also called Hickory Ridge. That's another spot where I met Stanley. The day after the testimonial dinner, they had a big barbeque at the house for him.

There were so many people vying for his attention, it was hard to get individual time with him. He was nice enough. He had a reputation for being real, real nice. Harry did not have the reputation of being the nice guy that Stanley was. He had some rough and tumble jobs after baseball. He owned a bar in Shamokin, and he was a cop in Shamokin for a while. He had a reputation for being a pretty rough, tough guy. Stanley was real mild compared to Harry.

When he was down there at the picnic they had for him, he had a big audience around him, and he was chewing the whole time.

I was at the parade. I was staying at my grandma's house. There were so many people trying to stay there that not everybody could, but I was one of the lucky ones. They had cots set up throughout the house for all these people to stay.

They gave him a key to the city.

There were some good memories. It was packed.

He was on the Ed Sullivan Show. Right after the induction, I guess he was doing a tour around the country. If you remember, he (Sullivan) used to have celebrities out in the audience, and he would introduce them from the audience. They didn't come up on stage. He introduced him and Frances in the audience.

I have a baseball that he sent to my father that I inherited from my father, signed by all Hall of Famers.[20]

Frank Kibler
Great nephew of Stan's wife, Frances.

My memory consists of fishing with the man after his baseball career. He used to have this half boat he'd put together. We'd fish for blue gill. Aunt Frances would fry them up.

He had a memento room that was about 8 x 10. He always had a spittoon. He chewed tobacco till the day he died.

We would go out there (South Bend), and he'd come to our house. Almost every year, he'd make a trip to the Hall of Fame to see his buddies, and then he'd stop in York. He would bring a baseball that was signed.

He was very quiet. He didn't have a lot of words to say. When he'd watch games, he'd always be yelling at the pitchers. That would be the only time he'd yell.

Back in the day, he was a big drinker. The whole family was. He always liked the beer. But I never saw him drink to excess.

Aunt Frances was a short lady and high energy, and she'd put him in his place. She ruled the roost.

He died without a lot of money. My mom always said if he was around today, he'd be a very wealthy man.[21]

Bob and Kathy Lavelle
Kathy is a great-niece of Stan's wife, Frances

Bob: When we got married. Uncle Stan and Aunt Frances came to the wedding. We expected our first child three years later. After Carrie, our daughter, was born, we wanted to get her baptized. Uncle Stan and Aunt Frances were there, and we got pictures of him holding Carrie.

When we lived in South Bend, we'd go over to his house, and he always had a spittoon to his right. Carrie was a toddler then. He and I were talking with my father-in-law Al. We were getting ready for early dinner. He had a bearskin rug on the floor with a head on it. Uncle Stan had his foot on the head of a bear, and Carrie was walking along the table, and he made a grrr sound, and it scared the shit out of Carrie. Aunt Frances smacked Uncle Stan and said you scared the hell out of that child. She's going to be scarred for life. She was a doll, but she didn't put up with that kind of crap. It just shows the family side of Uncle Stan and Aunt Frances. He was a jokester.

I used to go fishing with him on the weekends. He had a little boat and minnows.

When his first wife passed away, he knew Aunt Frances. He asked her to marry him, and he said, "We'll just keep it in the family."

Kathy: He had all the pennants on the wall.

My dad lived with Aunt Frances and Uncle Stan for two or three years and did work on their house

Bob: He was a quiet guy but very family-oriented. He was a down-home quiet man.[22]

Patricia Heisse
Great niece, granddaughter of Stan's brother Frank.

We to Shamokin when they had a big party for him. I was like 17-year-old, and my boyfriend and another couple went up with us to the party they had. He was a nice man, and my mom said he was one of the nicest people. He was the first one up there to get a car because he was a ballplayer.[23]

COVEY TIMELINE

July 13, 1889	Born in Shamokin
1909	Start of professional career with Lancaster Red Roses
September 10, 1912	Major-league debut with Philadelphia Athletics at Detroit
1913	Played for Spokane Indians for two seasons
February 11, 1915	Married Mary Shivetts
1915	Played for Portland Beavers and learned to throw spitball
November 27, 1916	Signed with Cleveland Indians
December 7, 1915	Son William born in Portland
April 11, 1917	Opening-day starter for Cleveland
May 24, 1918	Pitched 19 innings in 3-2 win over Yankees
August 24, 1919	Ray Caldwell hit by lightning, then finishes game
September 12, 1919	Son Jack born in Shamokin
February 9, 1920	Spitball outlawed at beginning of season
May 28, 1920	Wife Mary died in Shamokin
August 17, 1920	Ray Chapman died day after being hit by pitch by Carl Mays
October 5, 1920	Won Opening Game of World Series against Brooklyn
October 9, 1920	Won Game Four of World Series against Brooklyn
October 12, 1920	Won Game Seven to clinch World Series against Brooklyn
January 1, 1924	Married Frances Shivetts, sister of Mary
December 11, 1924	Traded to Washington Nationals
October 8, 1925	Lost Game Two in World Series against Pittsburgh
October 12, 1925	Lost Game Five in World Series against Pittsburgh
June 17, 1927	Released by Washington

July 9, 1927	Signed with New York Yankees but didn't pitch
December 21, 1927	Signed new contract with Yankees
August 3, 1928	Pitched last game of baseball career at age 39
April 1929	Relocated to South Bend
July 17, 1938	Son Jack died
July 3, 1969	Shamokin testimonial
July 28, 1969	Entered Hall of Fame
June 11, 1976	Inducted into Polish-American Hall of Fame
March 20, 1984	Died in South Bend at 94
August 22, 1985	Son William died
April 1987	Stadium named for him in South Bend
May 11, 1992	Wife Frances died
August 23, 1997	Monument dedicated in Shamokin

COVEY'S IMMEDIATE FAMILY

The following information was compiled from ancestry.com, geneologybank.com, and newspapers.com with tremendous help from Dr. Ann Yezerski, a genealogy whiz, whose family lived in Shamokin.

Stanislaus Anthony Kowalewski

Born July 13, 1889, in Fidler's Green section of Shamokin.
Changed name to Stanley Coveleski while playing baseball
After baseball career, moved to South Bend, Indiana, in 1929
Died March 20, 1984
Buried in St. Joseph Cemetery, South Bend.

First wife Mary Shivetts (sometimes Mae or May)

Born September 28, 1891
Married February 11, 1915
Died May 28, 1920 (age 28) when sons were 4 years and 8 months old
Cause of death was Pulmonary Tuberculosis, complicated by influenza

Living with her parents at 27 Vine St. at the time
Buried in St. Stanislaus Cemetery, Shamokin
Father was Joseph Shivetts (1860-1928)
Mother was Anna Tighe Shivetts (1873-1943)

Second wife Frances D. Shivetts

Sister of Stan's first wife
Born July 9, 1899
Married on January 1, 1924, in Uniontown, Coal Township
20 years old when Mary died
Died May 11, 1992
Buried in St. Joseph Cemetery, South Bend, Indiana

Son William E. Coveleski

Born December 7, 1915, in Portland, Oregon
Married Lucille A. Lucy Aranowski (1915-1994)
One son, John Joseph Coveleski (born and died September 27, 1948)
Died August 22, 1985
Buried in St. Joseph Cemetery, South Bend, Indiana

Son John J. "Jack" Coveleski

Born September 12, 1919, in Shamokin
Died July 17, 1938, in South Bend
Died from aortic dilatation of the heart and rheumatic endocarditis.
Buried in St. Stanislaus Cemetery, Shamokin

Father Anthony Kowalewski

Born May 4, 1846, in Poland
Married Anna Racicz in 1870
Immigrated to NYC circa 1873, then moved to Shamokin
Lived in Fidler's Green section of Shamokin
Worked as a coal miner at Luke Fidler Colliery for 40 years
Died March 19, 1929, in Shamokin
Buried in St. Stanislaus Cemetery, Shamokin

Mother Anna Racicz Kowalewski

Name may have been Antonina or Antonette
Born 1850 in Poland
Immigrated to U.S. circa 1873
Died January 24,1912, in Shamokin
Buried in St. Stanislaus Cemetery, Shamokin

Brother Jacob Kowalewski

Born about 1875 in Fidler's Green section of Shamokin
Died October 28, 1898, in Spanish-American War
Drowned; body lost at sea

Sister Sophia Glassic

Born March 4, 1879, in Fidler's Green section of Shamokin
Married John F. Glassic (Glassis, Glazik) in 1898
Mother of Walter Glassic, Ellen "Nellie" Honicker, Joseph Glassic,
    Michael Glassic, Herman Glassic, Mary Steele, Verna Amarose,
    Alberth Glassic, Louis Glassic, Thomas Glassic, Adam Glassic
    (twin), Eve Basile (twin), Stephen Glassic.
Died April 4,1947
Buried in St. Edwards Cemetery, Shamokin

Brother Francis Coveleskie (Frank)

Born December 3,1881, in Fidler's Green section of Shamokin
Married Elizabeth "Lizzie" Murray
Father of Leo Coveleskie, Elizabeth Fitzgee, Frank Coveleskie,
    Verna Gillard, Mary Montanye, Harry Coveleskie, John
    Coveleskie, William Coveleskie, Robert Coveleskie, Eleanor
    Coveleskie, Joseph Coveleskie, Stanley Coveleskie
Died May 4, 1956
Buried in St. Edwards Cemetery, Shamokin

Sister Margaret Mary Novey

Born June 15, 1882, in Fidler's Green section of Shamokin
Married John Novey

Mother of Frank Novey, Florence Novey, Agnes Ponto, John Novey Jr.
Died March 8, 1954
Buried in St. Stanislaus Cemetery, Shamokin

Brother John S. Coveleskie
Born November 9, 1884, in Fidler's Green section of Shamokin
Married Victoria Wieczorek
Father of John E. Coveleskie and Edward Cove
Died May 24, 1940
Buried in St. Stanislaus Cemetery, Shamokin

Brother Harry Frank Coveleski
Born April 23, 1886, in Fidler's Green section of Shamokin
Major-league baseball pitcher, 1907-1918, for the Philadelphia
     Phillies, Cincinnati Reds, and Detroit Tigers.
Married Celia (or Cecilia or Celie) Glassic, Sept. 17, 1913.
Adopted son William Birch (son of Celia's sister) in 1921
Owned "The Giant Killer" cafe, 602 Liberty Street, Shamokin
Died August 4, 1950, from cerebral hemorrhage
Buried in Saint Stanislaus Cemetery, Shamokin

Sister Helen E. Murawski
Born June 25, 1890, in Fidler's Green section of Shamokin
Married Michael Murawski (1886-1960)
Mother of Charles Murawski
Died May 14, 1958
Buried in Most Holy Redeemer Cemetery, Philadelphia
Father's name on death certificate was Antoni Kowalewski

COVEY AT A GLANCE

Throws right
Bats right
5-foot-11, 166 pounds

Career highlights

Won three games in 1920 World Series
Five 20-win seasons
Thirteen straight wins in 1925
Twenty-seven consecutive scoreless innings in 1923

Career numbers

14	Major-league seasons
*450	Games
385	Games started
223	Complete games
3,082	Innings pitched
215	Wins
142	Losses
.602	Winning percentage
38	Shutouts
2.89	Earned run average
3,055	Hits allowed
66	Home runs allowed
1,227	Runs allowed
990	Earned runs allowed
981	Strikeouts
802	Walks allowed
30	Hit batters
35	Wild pitches
1.251	WHIP
21	Saves
61.5	WAR

* Coveleski pitched in 450 games, but he played in 451. On June 27, 1917, he played right field at the end of the game in the Indians' 5-4 win over the St. Louis Browns at League Park. He did not bat in the game.

American League leader

Won-lost percentage	.800	1925	Washington
Earned run average	2.76	1923	Cleveland
	2.84	1925	Washington
Games started	40	1921	Cleveland
Shutouts	9	1917	Cleveland
	5	1923	Cleveland
Strikeouts	133	1920	Cleveland
Walks + hits per IP	1.108	1920	Cleveland .
Hits per 9 IP	6.094	1917	Cleveland
	8.114	1920	Cleveland

STAN'S SEASONS

Minor leagues

YEAR	TEAM	W	L	%	ERA	G	CG	SHO	IP	H	R	ER	HR	K	BB
1909	Lancaster	23	11	.676	1.95	43			272	225	84	59		68	
1910	Lancaster	15	8	.652	2.01	30			224	205	70	50		67	
1911	Lancaster	15	19	.441	2.81	36			272	288	120	85		65	
1912	Lanc./AC	20	14	.588	2.53	40			302	247	120	85		84	
1913	Spokane	17	20	.459	2.82	48			316	300	140	99		95	
1914	Spokane	20	15	.571		43			314	269	109			99	214
1915	Portland	17	17	.500	2.67	64			293	279	123	87		82	171

American League

YEAR	TEAM	W	L	%	ERA	G	CG	SHO	IP	H	R	ER	HR	BB	K
1912	Philadelphia	2	1	.667	3.43	5	2	1	21	18	9	8	0	4	9
1916	Cleveland	15	13	.536	3.41	45	11	1	232	247	100	88	6	58	76
1917	Cleveland	19	14	.576	1.81	45	24	**9**	298.1	202	78	60	3	94	133
1918	Cleveland	22	13	.629	1.82	38	25	2	311	261	90	63	2	76	87
1919	Cleveland	24	12	.667	2.61	43	24	4	286	**286**	99	83	2	60	118
1920	Cleveland	24	14	.632	2.49	41	26	3	315	284	110	87	6	65	**133**
1921	Cleveland	23	13	.639	3.37	**43**	28	2	315	341	137	118	6	84	99
1922	Cleveland	17	14	.548	3.32	35	21	3	276.2	292	120	102	14	64	98
1923	Cleveland	13	14	.481	2.76	33	16	**5**	228	251	98	70	8	42	54
1924	Cleveland	15	16	.484	4.04	37	18	2	240.1	286	140	108	6	73	58
1925	Washington	20	5	**.800**	**2.84**	32	15	3	241	230	86	76	7	73	58
1926	Washington	14	11	.560	3.12	36	11	3	245.1	272	112	85	1	81	50
1927	Washington	2	1	.667	3.14	5	0	0	14.1	13	7	5	0	8	3
1928	New York	5	1	.833	5.74	12	2	0	58	72	41	37	5	20	5
14-year totals		215	142	.602	2.89	*450	223	38	3082	3055	1227	990	66	802	981

(**Bold face:** League lead)

*Coveleski pitched in 450 games, but he played in 451. On June 27, 1917, he played right field at the end of the game in the Indians' 5-4 win over the St. Louis Browns at League Park. He did not bat in the game.

World Series

YEAR	OPPONENT	W	L	%	ERA	G	CG	SHO	IP	H	R	ER	HR	BB	K
1920	Brooklyn	3	0	1.000	0.67	3	3	1	27	15	2	2	0	2	8
1925	Pittsburgh	0	2	0.000	3.77	2	1	0	14.1	16	7	6	2	5	3
Totals		3	2	.600	1.74	5	4	1	41.1	31	9	8	2	7	11

NOTABLE BOX SCORES

First start
Philadelphia Athletics 3, Detroit Tigers 0
Thursday, September12, 1912
Navin Field, Detroit

	1	2	3	4	5	6	7	8	9	R	H	E
Philadelphia	1	0	0	0	0	1	0	1	0	3	7	2
Detroit	0	0	0	0	0	0	0	0	0	0	3	1

Philadelphia Athletics	AB	R	H	BI	BB	K
Eddie Murphy, RF	4	1	1	0	0	0
Harl Maggert, CF	1	2	0	0	2	1
Eddie Collins, 2B	4	0	1	1	0	1
Home Run Baker, 3B	4	0	2	2	0	0
Stuffy McInnis, 1B	3	0	1	0	1	0
Jimmy Walsh, LF	4	0	1	0	0	0
Jack Barry, SS	4	0	0	0	0	0
Ben Egan, C	4	0	1	0	0	1
Stan Coveleski, P	3	0	0	0	0	3
Totals	31	3	7	3	3	6

2B: Baker. LOB: 5. DP: 2. E: McInnis 2. SB: Maggert.

Detroit Tigers	AB	R	H	BI	BB	K
Donie Bush, SS	3	0	0	0	1	1
Red Corriden, 3B	4	0	0	0	0	0
Sam Crawford, RF	4	0	0	0	0	0
Ty Cobb, CF	3	0	1	0	0	0
Bobby Veach, LF	3	0	1	0	0	0
Baldy Louden, 2B	3	0	0	0	0	0
Eddie Onslow, 2B	3	0	1	0	0	0
Oscar Stanage, C	3	0	0	0	0	1
Charlie Wheatley, P	2	0	0	0	0	0
Dave Jones, PH	1	0	0	0	0	1
Tex Covington, P	0	0	0	0	0	0
Totals	29	0	3	0	1	3

2B: Cobb. LOB: 3. E: Stanage.

Philadelphia	IP	H	R	ER	BB	K
Stan Coveleski, W (1-0)	9	3	0	0	1	3

Detroit	IP	H	R	ER	BB	K
Charlie Wheatley, L (0-2)	8	6	3		3	6
Tex Covington	1	1	0	0	0	0

Time: 1:40. Attendance: 4,002.

19-inning game
Cleveland Indians 3, New York Yankees 2
Friday, May 24, 1918
Polo Grounds, New York

	1	2	3	4	5	6	7	8	9	10	11	12	13	14	15	16	17	18	19	R	H	E
Cleveland	0	0	1	0	0	0	1	0	0	0	0	0	0	0	0	0	0	0	1	3	15	1
New York	0	0	0	0	0	0	1	0	1	0	0	0	0	0	0	0	0	0	0	2	12	1

Cleveland Indians	AB	R	H	BI	BB	K
Ed Miller, 1B	7	0	1	0	1	0
Ray Chapman, SS	8	0	1	0	0	2
Tris Speaker, CF	8	0	2	0	0	0
Braggo Roth, RF	7	0	1	0	0	1
Bill Wambsganss, 2B	7	0	1	0	1	0
Smokey Joe Wood, LF	7	2	3	2	1	1
Al Halt, 3B	8	1	1	0	0	0
Steve O'Neill, C	7	0	4	0	1	0
Stan Coveleski, P	8	0	1	0	0	1
Totals	67	3	15	2	4	5

2B: Coveleski, O'Neill. HR: Wood 2. LOB: 12. With RISP: 0-for-9. E: Wambsganss. SB: O'Neill.

New York Yankees	AB	R	H	BI	BB	K
Frank Gilhooley, RF	9	0	3	0	0	0
Roger Peckinpaugh, SS	6	0	3	0	2	0
Home Run Baker, 3B	6	0	0	0	2	1
Del Pratt, 2B	8	0	1	0	0	1
Wally Pipp, 1B	7	1	2	0	1	0
Ping Bodie, LF	6	1	1	2	0	0
Elmer Miller, CF	8	0	2	0	0	0
Truck Hannah, C	2	0	0	0	1	0
Roxy Walters, PR-C	5	0	0	0	0	0
Allen Russell, P	2	0	0	0	0	0
Ray Caldwell, PH	1	0	0	0	0	1
George Mogridge, P	4	0	0	0	0	1
Armando Marsans, PH	1	0	0	0	0	0
Totals	65	2	12	2	6	4

3B: Pipp. HR: Bodie. LOB: 14. With RISP: 0-for-9. E: Pipp. SB: Pratt, Peckinpaugh.

Cleveland	IP	H	R	ER	BB	K
Stan Coveleski, W (6-3)	19	12	2	2	6	4

New York	IP	H	R	ER	BB	K
Allen Russell	7	7	2	1	2	3
George Mogridge, L (4-4)	12	8	1	1	2	2

IBB: Mogridge 1, Coveleski 2.

1920 World Series
Game One
Cleveland Indians 3, Brooklyn Robins 1
Tuesday, October 5, 1920
Ebbets Field, Brooklyn

	1	2	3	4	5	6	7	8	9	R	H	E
Cleveland	0	2	0	1	0	0	0	0	0	3	5	0
Brooklyn	0	0	0	0	0	0	1	0	0	1	5	1

Cleveland Indians	AB	R	H	BI	BB	K
Joe Evans, LF	2	0	0	0	1	0
Charlie Jamieson, PH-LF	1	0	0	0	0	0
Bill Wambsganss, 2B	3	0	0	0	0	1
Tris Speaker, CF	4	0	0	0	0	1
George Burns, 1B	3	1	1	0	0	1
Elmer Smith, PH-RF	1	0	0	0	0	0
Larry Gardner, 3B	4	0	0	0	0	0
Smokey Joe Wood, RF	2	2	1	0	1	1
Doc Johnston, PH-1B	1	0	0	0	0	0
Joe Sewell, SS	3	0	1	0	0	1
Steve O'Neill, C	3	0	2	2	0	1
Stan Coveleski, P	3	0	0	0	0	1
Totals	**30**	**3**	**5**	**2**	**2**	**7**

2B: O'Neill, Wod. LOB: 3. With RISP: 2-for-7.

Brooklyn Robins	AB	R	H	BI	BB	K
Ivy Olson, SS	3	0	2	0	1	0
Jimmy Johnston, 3B	3	0	0	0	0	1
Tommy Griffith, RF	4	0	1	0	0	0
Zack Wheat, LF	4	1	1	0	0	0
Hi Myers, CF	4	0	0	0	0	0
Ed Konetchy, 1B	4	0	0	1	0	1
Pete Kilduff, 2B	3	0	0	0	0	1
Ernie Krueger, C	3	0	0	0	0	0
Rube Marquard, P	1	0	0	0	0	0
Bill Lamar, PH	1	0	0	0	0	0
Al Mamaux, P	0	0	0	0	0	0
Clarence Mitchell, PH	1	0	1	0	0	0
Bernie Neis, PR	0	0	0	0	0	0
Leon Cadore, P	0	0	0	0	0	0
Totals	**31**	**1**	**5**	**1**	**1**	**3**

2B: Wheat. LOB: 5. With RISP: 0-for-7. E: Konetchy.

Cleveland	IP	H	R	ER	BB	K
Stan Coveleski, W (1-0)	9	5	3	1	1	3

Brooklyn	IP	H	R	ER	BB	K
Rube Marquard, L (0-1)	6	5	3	3	2	4
Al Mamaux	2	0	0	0	0	3
Leon Cadore	1	0	0	0	0	0

Time: 1:41. Attendance: 25,573.

Game Four
Cleveland Indians 5, Brooklyn Robins 1
Wednesday, October 9, 1920
League Park, Cleveland

	1	2	3	4	5	6	7	8	9	R	H	E
Brooklyn	0	0	0	1	0	0	0	0	0	1	5	1
Cleveland	2	0	2	0	0	1	0	0	x	5	12	2

Brooklyn Robins	AB	R	H	BI	BB	K
Ivy Olson, SS	4	0	1	0	0	0
Jimmy Johnston, 3B	4	1	2	0	0	0
Bernie Neis, PR	0	0	0	0	0	0
Tommy Griffith, RF	4	0	1	1	0	0
Zack Wheat, LF	4	0	0	0	0	0
Hi Myers, CF	3	0	0	0	0	1
Ed Konetchy, 1B	2	0	0	0	1	0
Pete Kilduff, 2B	3	0	1	0	0	2
Otto Miller, C	3	0	0	0	0	0
Leon Cadore, P	0	0	0	0	0	0
Al Mamaux, P	1	0	0	0	0	1
Rube Marquard, P	0	0	0	0	0	0
Bill Lamar, PH	1	0	0	0	0	0
Jeff Pfeffer, P	1	0	0	0	0	0
Totals	30	1	5	1	1	4

2B: Griffith. LOB: 3. With RISP: 0-for-2. DP: 1. PB: Miller. E: Wheat.

Cleveland Indians	AB	R	H	BI	BB	K
Charlie Jamieson, LF	2	0	0	0	0	0
Joe Evans, PH-LF	3	0	1	0	0	0
Bill Wambsganss, 2B	4	2	2	1	1	0
Tris Speaker, CF	5	2	2	0	0	0
Elmer Smith, RF	1	0	1	1	0	0
George Burns, PH-1B	2	0	1	2	1	1
Larry Gardner, 3B	3	0	1	1	0	1
Doc Johnston, 1B	1	0	0	0	0	1
Joe Wood, PH-RF	2	0	0	0	0	0
Jack Graney, PH-RF	1	0	0	0	0	0
Joe Sewell, SS	4	0	2	0	0	0
Steve O'Neill, C	2	0	1	0	2	1
Stan Coveleski, P	4	1	1	0	0	1
Totals	34	5	12	5	4	5

LOB: 10. With RISP: 5-for-15. DP: 2. E: Sewell, Burns.

Brooklyn	IP	H	R	ER	BB	K
Leon Cadore, L (0-1)	1	4	2	2	1	1
Al Mamaux	1	2	2	2	0	1
Rube Marquard	3	2	0	0	1	2
Jeff Pfeffer	3	4	1	1	2	1

Cleveland	IP	H	R	ER	BB	K
Stan Coveleski, W (2-0)	9	5	1	1	1	4

WP: Pfeffer. IBB: Marquard, Pfeffer.
Time: 1:54. Attendance: 25,734.

Game Seven

Cleveland Indians 3, Brooklyn Robins 0
Wednesday, October 12, 1920
League Park, Cleveland

	1	2	3	4	5	6	7	8	9	R	H	E
Brooklyn	0	0	0	0	0	0	0	0	0	0	5	2
Cleveland	0	0	0	1	1	0	1	0	x	3	7	3

Brooklyn Robins	AB	R	H	BI	BB	K
Ivy Olson, SS	4	0	0	0	0	0
Jack Sheehan, 3B	4	0	1	0	0	0
Tommy Griffith, RF	4	0	0	0	0	0
Zack Wheat, LF	4	0	2	0	0	0
Hi Myers, CF	4	0	0	0	0	0
Ed Konetchy, 1B	4	0	1	0	0	0
Pete Kilduff, 2B	3	0	0	0	0	0
Otto Miller, C	2	0	0	0	0	1
Bill Lamar, PH	1	0	0	0	0	0
Ernie Krueger, C	0	0	0	0	0	0
Burleigh Grimes, P	2	0	1	0	0	0
Ray Schmandt, PH	1	0	0	0	0	0
Al Mamaux, P	0	0	0	0	0	0
Totals	33	0	5	0	0	1

LOB: 6. With RISP: 1-for-3. E: Sheehan, Grimes.

Cleveland Indians	AB	R	H	BI	BB	K
Charlie Jamieson, LF	4	1	2	1	0	0
Bill Wambsganss, 2B	4	0	1	0	0	0
Tris Speaker, CF	3	0	1	1	1	0
Elmer Smith, RF	3	0	0	0	1	0
Larry Gardner, 3B	4	1	1	0	0	0
Doc Johnston, 1B	2	0	1	0	2	0
Joe Sewell, SS	4	0	0	0	0	0
Steve O'Neill, C	4	0	1	0	0	1
Stan Coveleski, P	3	1	0	0	0	2
Totals	31	3	7	2	4	3

2B: O'Neill, Jamieson. 3B: Speaker. LOB: 8. With RISP: 2-for-10. E: Sewell 2, Coveleski. SB: Johnston, Jamieson.

Brooklyn	IP	H	R	ER	BB	K
Burleigh Grimes, L (1-2)	7	7	3	2	4	2
Al Mamaux	1	0	0	0	0	1

Cleveland	IP	H	R	ER	BB	K
Stan Coveleski, W (3-0)	9	5	0	0	0	1

Time: 1:55. Attendance: 27,525.

1925 World Series
Game Two
Pittsburgh Pirates 3, Washington Nationals 2
Tuesday, October 8, 1925
Forbes Field, Pittsburgh

	1	2	3	4	5	6	7	8	9	R	H	E
Washington	0	1	0	0	0	0	0	0	1	2	8	2
Pittsburgh	0	0	0	1	0	0	0	2	x	3	7	0

Washington Nationals	AB	R	H	BI	BB	K
Sam Rice, CF	5	0	2	0	0	0
Bucky Harris, 2B	3	0	0	0	0	1
Goose Goslin, LF	4	0	0	0	0	0
Joe Judge, 1B	4	1	1	1	0	0
Joe Harris, RF	3	0	2	0	1	0
Earl McNeely, PR	0	1	0	0	0	0
Ossie Bluege, 3B	2	0	0	0	0	0
Buddy Myer, PR-3B	1	0	1	0	0	0
Roger Peckinpaugh, SS	3	0	1	0	1	0
Muddy Ruel, C	3	0	1	0	0	1
Bobby Veach, PH	0	0	0	1	0	0
Stan Coveleski, P	2	0	0	0	0	1
Dutch Ruether, PH	1	0	0	0	0	1
Totals	31	2	8	2	2	4

HR: Judge. SF: Veach. HBP: Bluege. LOB: 8. With RISP: 0-for-8. PB: Ruel. E: Peckinpaugh.

Pittsburgh Pirates	AB	R	H	BI	BB	K
Eddie Moore, 2B	4	1	0	0	0	1
Max Carey, CF	4	0	2	0	0	1
Kiki Cuyler, RF	3	1	1	2	0	0
Clyde Barnhart, LF	4	0	1	0	0	0
Pie Traynor, 3B	3	0	0	0	1	0
Glenn Wright, SS	4	1	2	1	0	0
George Grantham, 1B	4	0	0	0	0	0
Earl Smith, C	3	0	1	0	0	1
Vic Aldridge, P	3	0	0	0	0	0
Totals	32	3	7	3	1	3

HR: Wright, Cuyler. LOB: 7. With RISP: 1-for-7.

Washington	IP	H	R	ER	BB	K
Stan Coveleski, L (0-1)	8	7	3	2	1	3

Pittsburgh	IP	H	R	ER	BB	K
Vic Aldridge, W (1-0)	9	8	2	2	2	4

Balk: Aldridge. HBP: Aldridge.
Time: 2:04. Attendance: 43,364.

Game Five
Pittsburgh 6, Washington Nationals 3
Monday, October 12, 1925
Griffith Stadium, Washington

	1	2	3	4	5	6	7	8	9	R	H	E
Pittsburgh	0	0	2	0	0	0	2	1	1	6	13	0
Washington	1	0	0	1	0	0	1	0	0	3	8	1

Pittsburgh Pirates	AB	R	H	BI	BB	K
Eddie Moore, 2B	4	1	1	0	1	0
Max Carey, CF	4	2	2	0	1	0
Kiki Cuyler, RF	4	1	2	1	1	0
Clyde Barnhart, LF	4	1	2	2	1	0
Pie Traynor, 3B	3	0	1	1	1	1
Glenn Wright, SS	5	1	2	1	0	0
Stuffy McInnis, 1B	5	0	1	1	0	0
Earl Smith, C	3	0	2	0	0	0
Vic Aldridge, P	4	0	0	0	0	0
Totals	36	6	13	6	5	1

2B: Wright. SF: Traynor. LOB: 10. With RISP: 5-for-12. DP: 1. SB: Carey, Barnhart.

Washington Nationals	AB	R	H	BI	BB	K
Sam Rice, CF	5	1	2	1	0	0
Bucky Harris, 2B	3	0	0	0	0	0
Goose Goslin, LF	4	0	1	1	0	0
Joe Judge, 1B	3	0	0	0	1	1
Joe Harris, RF	3	1	2	1	1	0
Roger Peckinpaugh, SS	3	0	0	0	0	1
Muddy Ruel, C	3	0	1	0	1	0
Ossie Bluege, 3B	4	0	1	0	0	2
Stan Coveleski, P	1	0	0	0	1	1
Win Ballou, P	0	0	0	0	0	0
Nemo Leibold, PH	1	1	1	0	0	0
Tom Zachary, P	0	0	0	0	0	0
Firpo Marberry, P	0	0	0	0	0	0
Spencer Adams, PH	1	0	0	0	0	0
Totals	31	3	8	3	4	5

2B: Goslin, Bluege, Leibold. HR: Harris. LOB: 8. With RISP: 2-for-9. DP: 2. E: Peckinpaugh.

Pittsburgh	IP	H	R	ER	BB	K
Vic Aldridge, W (2-0)	9	8	3	3	4	5

Washington	IP	H	R	ER	BB	K
Stan Coveleski, L (0-2)	6.1	9	4	4	4	0
Win Ballou	0.2	0	0	0	0	1

Washington	IP	H	R	ER	BB	K
Tom Zachary	1.2	3	2	2	1	0
Firpo Marberry	0.1	1	0	0	0	0

Time: 2:26. Attendance: 35,899.

Final game
St. Louis Browns 8, New York Yankees 0
Friday, August 3, 1928
Sportsman's Park, St. Louis

	1	2	3	4	5	6	7	8	9	R	H	E
New York	0	0	0	0	0	0	0	0	0	0	6	3
St. Louis	0	1	0	2	1	1	3	0	x	8	11	0

New York Yankees	AB	R	H	BI	BB	K
Earle Combs, CF	3	0	1	0	1	0
Mark Koenig, SS	4	0	0	0	0	1
Babe Ruth, LF	4	0	0	0	0	1
Lou Gehrig, 1B	2	0	1	0	2	0
Bob Meusel, RF	4	0	0	0	0	0
Gene Robertson, 3B	4	0	2	0	0	0
Leo Durocher, 2B	4	0	1	0	0	1
Johnny Grabowski, C	2	0	0	0	0	1
Cedric Durst, PH	1	0	0	0	0	0
Pat Collins, C	0	0	0	0	0	0
Waite Hoyt, P	2	0	0	0	0	0
Stan Coveleski, P	0	0	0	0	0	0
Myles Thomas, P	1	0	1	0	0	0
Totals	31	0	6	0	3	4

LOB: 7. With RISP: 0-for-7. E: Koenig 2, Combs. SB: Robertson.

St. Louis Browns	AB	R	H	BI	BB	K
Earl McNeely, RF	4	1	1	0	0	0
Otis Brannan, 2B	4	0	0	0	1	0
Heinie Manush, LF	5	1	1	0	0	1
Fred Schulte, CF	3	1	2	2	0	0
Red Kress, SS	4	1	0	0	0	0
Lu Blue, 1B	3	4	2	2	1	0
Frank O'Rourke, 3B	3	0	3	3	0	0
Wally Schang, C	3	0	0	0	1	0
Sam Gray, P	4	0	2	1	0	0
Totals	33	8	11	8	3	1

2B: O'Rourke. 3B: O'Rourke, Manush, Blue. SF: Schulte. LOB: 7. With RISP: 5-for-12. DP: 2. SB: Blue 2.

New York	IP	H	R	ER	BB	K
Waite Hoyt, L (13-3)	5	6	4	3	1	1
Stan Coveleski	1.2	4	4	1	2	0
Myles Thomas	1.1	1	0	0	0	0

St. Louis	IP	H	R	ER	BB	K
Sam Gray, W (16-8)	9	6	0	0	3	4

Time: 2:07. Attendance: 4,000.

COVEY'S 450 GAMES

1912 Philadelphia Athletics

DATE	OPPONENT	SCORE	DECISION	IP	H	R	ER	BB	K
September									
10	@ Detroit	L 6-8		1	0	0	0	1	0
11	@ Detroit	W 9-7		0	0	0	0	1	0
12	@ Detroit	W 3-0	W (1-0) SHO	9	3	0	0	1	3
18	@ Chicago	L 1-9	L (1-1) CG	8	14	9	8	1	3
30	New York	W 11-10	W (2-1)	3	1	0	0	0	3

1916 Cleveland Indians

DATE	OPPONENT	SCORE	DECISION	IP	H	R	ER	BB	K
April									
13	St. Louis	L 2-4		1	2	0	0	0	1
17	Detroit	L 1-3	L (0-1) CG	12	13	3	3	2	6
21	@ St. Louis	L 1-11		2	3	1	0	0	0
26	Chicago	W 5-3	W (1-1)	8	9	2	2	1	1
29	@ Detroit	L 4-5	L (1-2)	2.1	3	1	1	2	2
May									
1	@ Detroit	W 2-0	W (2-2) SHO	5	2	0	0	1	1
5	@ Chicago	W 3-2	W (3-2) CG	9	7	2	2	3	3
9	@ Boston	L 1-5	L (3-3)	7	5	3	2	2	2
13	@ New York	W 4-2	W (4-3) CG	9	7	2	2	2	6
18	@ Washington	W 4-2	W (5-3)	6.1	9	2	2	3	1
21	Washington	L 3-4		8	7	3	2	3	3
28	@ Chicago	L 0-2		1	0	0	0	0	0
30	@ St. Louis	L 4-5		9.1	7	4	4	1	6
June									
3	Boston	W 11-2	W (6-3) CG	9	7	2	2	0	5
8	Washington	T 5-5		1	5	5	3	1	1
10	Philadelphia	W 10-1	W (7-3) CG	9	8	1	1	0	3
12	Philadelphia	W 3-1	S (1)	1	0	0	0	0	3
15	New York	W 3-2	W (8-3) CG	10	10	2	2	2	1
17	New York	L 3-5		2	2	1	1	0	0

DATE	OPPONENT	SCORE		DECISION		IP	H	R	ER	BB	K
19	New York	L	6-7	L	(8-4)	8	11	7	7	4	4
22	@ Detroit	W	4-3			7	5	2	2	0	2
24	@ Detroit	W	10-8			5.2	10	5	5	3	0
28	Chicago	L	1-5	L	(8-5)	7	7	3	3	0	0
July											
1	St. Louis	W	5-4	W	(9-5)	5	0	0	0	0	1
4	Detroit	W	6-3	W	(10-5) CG	9	11	3	1	2	3
8	@ Boston	W	5-1	W	(11-5) CG	9	5	1	1	6	0
10	@ New York	W	3-2	S	(2)	2	1	0	0	2	2
12	@ New York	W	6-3	S	(3)	1.1	1	0	0	0	1
13	@ New York	L	3-6			2.2	3	2	1	3	1
16	Washington	L	2-4	L	(11-6) CG	9	10	4	4	3	3
27	Boston	L	6-7	L	(11-7)	7	10	6	3	1	0
30	Washington	L	1-2	L	(11-8)	1.1	2	1	1	0	0
August											
1	Washington	W	6-1	W	(12-8) CG	9	9	1	0	0	2
5	Philadelphia	W	12-3	W	(13-8)	5	6	3	3	2	2
9	New York	W	5-3	W	(14-8)	7	9	3	3	1	1
11	@ St. Louis	L	4-5	L	(14-9)	2.1	4	2	2	1	1
17	@ New York	L	4-5			7.2	13	4	4	1	2
23	@ Boston	L	3-7	L	(14-10)	3	4	4	4	2	0
24	@ Philadelphia	L	5-6			2	4	1	1	0	2
26	@ Philadelphia	L	0-5	L	(14-11)	5	7	5	5	1	2
30	@ Washington	L	1-3			2	1	1	1	0	0
September											
2	St. Louis	W	5-4	W	(15-11)	1.1	0	0	0	0	0
4	@ Detroit	L	5-7	L	(15-12)	0.2	4	5	5	2	1
6	@ Chicago	L	3-4			0.2	1	0	0	1	1
12	Detroit	L	2-10	L	(15-13)	0.1	3	3	3	1	0

1917 Cleveland Indians

DATE	OPPONENT	SCORE		DECISION		IP	H	R	ER	BB	K
April											
11	@ Detroit	W	6-4	W	(1-0) CG	9	8	4	4	2	2
15	@ St. Louis	W	4-0	W	(2-0)	9	5	0	0	2	6
19	Detroit	W	8-7			3	5	4	4	2	3
24	@ Chicago	L	1-0	L	(2-1) CG	8.1	2	1	1	2	3
27	@ Chicago	W	2-1	S	(1)	1	0	0	0	0	2
29	St. Louis	L	5-6	L	(2-2)	1	3	2	1	1	2
30	St. Louis	L	2-4			5	6	2	1	1	3
May											
8	@ Detroit	W	5-2	W	(3-2) CG	9	3	2	1	3	6
13	Washington	W	2-0	W	(4-2) SHO	9	5	0	0	3	3
17	Boston	W	7-1	W	(5-2) CG	9	6	1	1	1	3
24	New York	W	2-0	W	(6-2) SHO	9	4	0	0	5	4
29	Detroit	W	1-0	W	(7-2) SHO	10	7	0	0	2	2
June											
4	@ Boston	L	1-2	L	(7-3) CG	8	7	2	2	1	4
9	@ New York	W	2-0	W	(8-3) SHO	9	5	0	0	3	3

DATE	OPPONENT	SCORE		DECISION		IP	H	R	ER	BB	K
13	@ Washington	L	5-7	L	(8-4)	3	5	5	5	4	0
15	@ Philadelphia	L	2-3	L	(8-5) CG	8	7	3	2	0	3
20	@ Chicago	L	2-3	L	(8-6)	7	3	3	2	3	1
23	@ Chicago	L	1-2			3.2	0	0	0	0	1
25	St. Louis	W	9-6	W	(9-6) CG	9	9	6	2	4	8
26	St. Louis	W	6-2	S	(2)	1	1	0	0	0	0
29	Chicago	L	1-3	L	(9-7) CG	9	7	3	3	2	3
July											
3	@ St. Louis	L	4-5	L	(9-8) CG	8	10	5	5	5	3
5	@ St. Louis	W	5-3	S	(3)	0.1	1	0	0	0	0
7	Boston	W	3-1	W	(10-8) CG	9	3	1	1	1	4
11	Washington	W	3-0	W	(11-8) SHO	9	4	0	0	3	6
15	New York	L	0-4	L	(11-9)	8	9	4	4	1	4
18	New York	L	7-12	L	(11-10)	3	8	5	0	0	1
24	@ Washington	L	1-2	L	(11-11)	7	2	2	1	3	4
28	@ Washington	L	4-5			7	9	4	4	4	2
August											
1	@ Philadelphia	W	6-5	S	(4)	2.2	0	0	0	1	1
4	@ Boston	L	2-3	L	(11-12) CG	10.1	6	3	3	5	2
8	@ New York	W	2-1	W	(12-12) CG	9	5	1	1	2	3
10	@ New York	W	8-7	W	(13-12)	7	3	0	0	1	5
14	Chicago	L	2-3	L	(13-13) CG	9	4	3	3	2	2
18	Boston	W	2-1	W	(14-13) CG	9	7	1	1	3	4
22	Philadelphia	W	6-5			1	0	0	0	1	0
25	New York	L	0-3	L	(14-14)	8	4	2	2	3	8
27	Washington	L	9-11			4	2	1	1	3	4
31	Detroit	W	1-0	W	(15-14) SHO	9	6	0	0	3	4
September											
3	St. Louis	W	7-6			9	11	6	5	2	1
9	@ Chicago	L	3-3*			0	0	1	1	1	0
11	@ Detroit	W	1-0	W	(16-14) SHO	9	3	0	0	4	4
15	@ St. Louis	W	5-4	W	(17-14)	1	2	1	1	1	0
19	@ New York	W	2-0	W	(18-14) SHO	9	1	0	0	2	5
22	@ Philadelphia	W	2-1	W	(19-14) CG	11	4	1	0	3	5

* Coveleski started and walked the only batter he faced. Chicago was awarded the win by forfeit after the ninth inning because Cleveland was accused of delaying the game over a protested call at third base.

1918 Cleveland Indians

DATE	OPPONENT	SCORE		DECISION		IP	H	R	ER	BB	K
April											
18	Detroit	W	6-2	W	(1-0) CG	9	6	2	2	5	4
22	St. Louis	W	8-1	W	(2-0) CG	9	5	1	1	0	4
27	@ Detroit	W	3-2	W	(3-0) CG	12	8	2	2	5	2
May											
1	Chicago	W	6-5	W	(4-0) CG	9	9	5	0	2	1
5	@ St. Louis	L	0-3	L	(4-1)	7	10	3	3	0	3
8	@ Chicago	L	5-9			1	3	2	1	0	0
10	@ Washington	W	8-2	W	(5-1) CG	8	8	2	1	0	3
15	@ Philadelphia	L	2-3	L	(5-2) CG	12.2	9	3	3	3	10

DATE	OPPONENT	SCORE	DECISION	IP	H	R	ER	BB	K
19	@ Washington	L 0-1	L (5-3) CG	11.2	7	1	1	2	1
24	@ New York	W 3-2	W (6-3) CG	19	12	2	2	6	4
30	Chicago	W 3-2	W (7-3) CG	9	7	2	0	4	4
June									
3	Washington	L 2-3	L (7-4) CG	7	7	3	1	0	3
6	Boston	L 0-1	L (7-5) CG	10	3	1	0	6	5
9	Boston	L 0-2	L (7-6)	7	8	2	2	0	2
13	New York	L 2-3	L (7-7) CG	10	11	3	2	1	2
17	Philadelphia	W 6-3	W (8-7) CG	9	6	3	2	0	7
20	@ Chicago	L 4-5	L (8-8)	3.1	5	2	2	2	2
22	@ Chicago	W 4-3	W (9-8) CG	9	8	3	2	1	2
25	@ St. Louis	L 2-3		0.1	1	0	0	1	0
26	@ St. Louis	W 5-4	W (10-8)	8.1	6	4	4	3	1
30	Detroit	L 2-10	L (10-9)	7	12	9	7	1	2
July									
4	St. Louis	W 4-2	W (11-9) CG	9	10	2	2	1	3
8	@ Boston	L 0-1	L (11-10) CG	9.1	8	1	1	6	1
11	@ New York	W 1-0	W (12-10) SHO	9	3	0	0	2	1
15	@ New York	W 5-3	W (13-10) CG	9	7	3	3	3	1
18	@ Washington	W 5-1	W (14-10) CG	9	6	1	1	2	2
21	Philadelphia	W 3-2	W (15-10) CG	11	8	2	2	0	2
26	New York	W 8-3	W (16-10) CG	9	8	3	1	1	3
August									
2	Boston	W 6-3	W (17-10) CG	9	7	3	3	3	2
4	Boston	W 2-0	W (18-10) SHO	6	4	0	0	2	0
8	Washington	W 8-4	W (19-10)	7.2	10	4	4	4	2
11	Chicago	L 3-6	L (19-11)	4	6	3	3	0	1
15	@ New York	L 2-3	L (19-12) CG	8	6	3	2	1	1
19	@ Boston	L 0-6	L (19-13)	5	8	4	4	4	2
21	@ Washington	W 5-3	S (1)	4	2	1	1	0	2
23	@ Washington	W 6-2	W (20-13)	7	9	2	2	2	3
27	@ Philadelphia	W 8-6	W (21-13)	5	4	2	0	1	2
30	@ Detroit	W 2-1	W (22-13) CG	9	4	1	0	0	1

1919 Cleveland Indians

DATE	OPPONENT	SCORE	DECISION	IP	H	R	ER	BB	K
April									
25	@ Detroit	L 2-4	L (0-1)	7	10	4	2	2	0
May									
1	Detroit	L 1-8	L (0-2)	4	11	6	5	1	0
4	Detroit	W 5-4	W (1-2) CG	9	7	4	2	2	5
8	Chicago	L 1-4	L (1-3) CG	9	10	4	4	1	3
12	@ Detroit	W 6-4	S (1)	2.1	2	0	0	0	0
13	@ Detroit	W 8-5	S (2)	3.2	2	0	0	1	2
15	Washington	W 6-3	S (3)	1	0	0	0	0	0
18	New York	W 4-3	W (2-3) CG	9	9	3	3	0	5
22	Philadelphia	W 3-2	W (3-3) CG	10	6	2	1	0	4
26	Boston	W 12-7	W (4-3)	6	9	4	4	1	3
30	@ Chicago	L 2-3		7	5	2	2	2	0

DATE	OPPONENT	SCORE	DECISION	IP	H	R	ER	BB	K
June									
2	St. Louis	W 6-3		4	5	1	0	0	1
7	@ Philadelphia	W 3-2	W (5-3) CG	9	9	2	2	1	2
12	@ Washington	W 5-1	W (6-3) CG	9	7	1	1	1	3
16	@ Boston	W 1-0	W (7-3) SHO	9	3	0	0	2	2
19	@ New York	W 4-3	W (8-3) CG	9	7	3	3	3	3
24	@ Chicago	W 2-0	W (9-3) SHO	9	6	0	0	1	2
28	@ Detroit	L 1-3	L (9-4)	6	5	3	3	4	5
July									
2	Chicago	L 4-6		1.1	6	4	4	1	0
4	St. Louis	W 11-1	W (10-4) CG	9	10	1	1	3	4
7	@ St. Louis	L 2-3	L (10-5)	1.1	1	1	1	3	1
9	New York	W 2-0	W (11-5) SHO	9	7	0	0	0	3
13	Washington	W 5-4	W (12-5) CG	9	10	4	2	2	3
19	Boston	W 7-4	W (13-5) CG	9	12	4	4	4	2
22	Philadelphia	W 4-3	S (4)	0.2	0	0	0	0	0
24	Detroit	L 2-4	L (13-6) CG	9	11	4	3	1	3
27	Detroit	L 1-2	L (13-7)	1	2	1	1	0	0
29	@ Philadelphia	W 8-2	W (14-7) CG	9	7	2	2	0	3
August									
3	@ Washington	W 4-0	W (15-7) SHO	9	5	0	0	3	7
8	@ Boston	W 5-4	W (16-7) CG	9	7	4	4	5	4
12	@ New York	W 2-1	W (17-7) CG	9	6	1	1	0	2
15	Washington	L 2-3	L (17-8)	1.2	1	1	1	1	0
17	New York	L 2-6	L (17-9)	1	5	3	3	0	0
19	New York	W 5-1	W (18-9) CG	9	3	1	1	1	5
23	Philadelphia	W 6-2	W (19-9) CG	9	8	2	2	1	6
27	Detroit	W 7-5	W (20-9)	7	14	5	5	1	5
31	Chicago	W 6-1	W (21-9) CG	9	6	1	1	4	6
September									
3	@ St. Louis	L 5-6	L (21-10)	6.1	8	1	0	1	3
7	@ Chicago	L 3-8	L (21-11)	1.1	4	4	4	3	0
12	@ Boston	W 4-3	W (22-11) CG	9	7	3	3	2	5
16	@ Philadelphia	W 8-2	W (23-11) CG	9	11	2	2	0	5
20	@ Washington	W 6-3	W (24-11) CG	9	10	3	3	3	5
28	St. Louis	L 5-8	L (24-12)	7	12	8	3	0	6

1920 Cleveland Indians

DATE	OPPONENT	SCORE	DECISION	IP	H	R	ER	BB	K
April									
14	St. Louis	W 5-0	W (1-0) SHO	9	5	0	0	2	7
18	Detroit	W 11-4	W (2-0) CG	9	11	4	4	1	3
22	@ St. Louis	W 11-3	W (3-0)	7	5	3	1	1	2
27	Chicago	W 3-2	W (4-0) CG	9	7	2	2	2	3
May									
1	@ Detroit	W 9-3	W (5-0) CG	9	10	3	3	0	7
5	@ Chicago	W 3-2	W (6-0) CG	9	9	2	1	2	3
9	@ Chicago	W 4-3	W (7-0) CG	9	11	3	2	1	0
15	@ New York	L 0-2	L (7-1) CG	8	4	2	2	2	9
19	@ New York	W 5-0	W (8-1) SHO	9	6	0	0	1	2

DATE	OPPONENT	SCORE		DECISION		IP	H	R	ER	BB	K
23	Philadelphia	L	1-2	L	(8-2) CG	9	10	2	0	0	4
June											
6	St. Louis	L	2-6	L	(8-3)	7	11	6	4	3	2
10	Philadelphia	W	7-2	W	(9-3) CG	9	7	2	2	1	4
14	New York	W	7-1	W	(10-3) CG	9	5	1	0	6	4
19	Washington	L	1-3	L	(10-4)	7	7	3	1	0	7
25	@ Chicago	L	3-6	L	(10-5)	6	7	6	5	2	1
28	@ St. Louis	W	7-4	W	(11-5) CG	9	9	4	4	2	0
29	@ St. Louis	W	9-6	S	(1)	1.2	1	0	0	1	1
July											
2	@ Detroit	W	10-3	W	(12-5) CG	9	9	3	0	1	1
4	@ Detroit	W	11-3	W	(13-5)	2.1	0	0	0	0	0
5	@ Chicago	L	5-6	L	(13-6) CG	8	11	6	6	1	2
10	@ Washington	W	7-2	W	(14-6) CG	9	6	2	1	2	3
14	@ Philadelphia	W	5-3	W	(15-6) CG	9	8	3	3	0	2
19	@ Boston	W	10-6			6.1	10	6	6	1	1
22	@ New York	L	3-11	L	(15-7)	1	5	5	4	1	2
25	Chicago	W	7-2	W	(16-7) CG	9	9	2	2	3	6
29	Boston	W	9-3	W	(17-7) CG	9	9	3	3	2	3
August											
2	Washington	W	2-0	W	(18-7) SHO	9	5	0	0	2	6
6	Philadelphia	L	1-2	L	(18-8) CG	10	5	2	1	0	5
12	New York	L	1-5	L	(18-9)	7	5	5	4	3	5
16	@ New York	W	4-3	W	(19-9) CG	9	7	3	3	2	4
21	@ Boston	L	0-4	L	(19-10)	7	8	4	4	3	2
25	@ Philadelphia	L	1-2	L	(19-11)	7	8	2	2	0	2
29	@ Washington	L	2-3	L	(19-12)	8	8	3	2	6	3
September											
3	Detroit	L	0-1	L	(19-13) CG	9	5	1	1	1	2
9	New York	W	10-4	W	(20-13) CG	9	6	4	4	4	2
13	Philadelphia	W	3-2	W	(21-13) CG	9	6	2	2	2	5
17	Washington	W	9-3	W	(22-13) CG	9	7	3	3	2	8
21	Boston	W	12-1	W	(23-13)	8	7	1	1	0	3
25	Chicago	L	1-5	L	(23-14)	5	6	5	3	0	1
26	@ St. Louis	W	7-5	S	(2)	1.2	1	0	0	0	0
29	@ St. Louis	W	10-2	W	(24-14) CG	9	8	2	1	2	6

1921 Cleveland Indians

DATE	OPPONENT	SCORE		DECISION		IP	H	R	ER	BB	K
April											
13	@ St. Louis	L	2-4	L	(0-1)	7	5	4	3	2	4
14	@ St. Louis	W	12-9	S	(1)	2	1	0	0	0	0
19	@ Detroit	W	12-3	W	(1-1) CG	9	9	3	3	2	0
23	St. Louis	W	6-2	W	(2-1) CG	9	9	2	2	4	4
27	Detroit	L	2-5	L	(2-2) CG	10	14	5	5	5	0
May											
1	@ Chicago	W	5-1	W	(3-2) CG	9	6	1	1	1	1
6	Chicago	W	8-0	W	(4-2) SHO	9	6	0	0	1	3
11	Washington	W	14-1	W	(5-2) CG	9	4	1	0	0	4
15	New York	L	2-8	L	(5-3)	3	7	5	4	1	3

DATE	OPPONENT	SCORE	DECISION	IP	H	R	ER	BB	K
18	Philadelphia	W 4-2	W (6-3) CG	9	9	2	2	2	3
22	Boston	W 5-0	W (7-3) SHO	9	7	0	0	2	0
26	@ St. Louis	W 12-5	W (8-3) CG	8	10	5	3	4	1
30	@ Detroit	W 6-5	W (9-3) CG	9	9	5	5	5	4
June									
3	@ Boston	L 6-7		5	8	4	3	0	0
7	@ New York	L 2-9	L (9-4)	3.1	7	8	5	4	0
8	@ New York	L 3-4		0.1	1	0	0	1	0
11	@ Washington	W 7-3	W (10-4) CG	9	7	3	1	2	3
13	@ Washington	W 10-6	S (2)	3	2	0	0	1	3
15	@ Philadelphia	W 6-5	W (11-4) CG	11	16	5	5	3	4
19	Detroit	W 8-7		4	8	5	4	1	0
23	@ Chicago	L 0-6	L (11-5)	6.2	12	6	6	2	0
28	St. Louis	W 12-4	W (12-5) CG	9	17	4	4	2	1
July									
3	Detroit	W 9-5	W (13-5)	8.1	11	5	5	1	3
7	Philadelphia	L 3-5	L (13-6) CG	9	10	5	5	1	2
12	Boston	W 7-1	W (14-6) CG	9	7	1	1	2	4
16	Washington	W 8-4	W (15-6) CG	9	16	4	4	2	4
20	New York	L 1-7	L (15-7)	7	8	7	7	3	1
26	@ Boston	W 8-2	W (16-7) CG	10	5	2	2	2	2
30	@ New York	W 16-1	W (17-7) CG	9	7	1	1	2	4
August									
4	@ Washington	L 1-3	L (17-8) CG	8	12	3	3	0	2
8	@ Philadelphia	W 4-3	W (18-8) CG	9	9	3	3	0	5
12	Chicago	W 6-1	W (19-8) CG	9	7	1	1	1	1
17	Philadelphia	W 15-8		1.1	5	5	4	0	0
20	Boston	W 7-3	W (20-8) CG	9	10	3	1	3	2
24	New York	L 2-3	L (20-9) CG	9	9	3	2	6	7
28	Washington	W 3-2	W (21-9) CG	9	7	2	2	2	6
September									
1	@ Detroit	L 6-7		3	4	3	3	1	2
10	@ St. Louis	L 0-2	L (21-10)	7	7	2	2	1	4
14	@ Philadelphia	W 8-5	W (22-10) CG	9	9	5	2	0	8
18	@ Washington	L 1-4	L (22-11) CG	8	7	4	4	6	4
23	@ New York	L 2-4	L (22-12) CG	8	6	4	4	3	1
26	@ New York	L 7-8	L (22-13)	2.1	5	4	4	2	2
30	@ Chicago	W 3-2	W (23-13) CG	9	7	2	2	2	2

1922 Cleveland Indians

DATE	OPPONENT	SCORE	DECISION	IP	H	R	ER	BB	K
April									
13	Detroit	W 8-3		7	8	2	2	3	2
19	St. Louis	L 1-15	L (0-1)	7	12	6	4	1	3
23	@ Detroit	L 3-4	L (0-2) CG	8	7	4	4	2	1
29	@ St. Louis	L 5-6	L (0-3) CG	9.2	14	6	5	3	4
May									
2	@ Chicago	W 10-6	W (1-3) CG	9	11	6	6	3	1
6	St. Louis	W 6-2	W (2-3) CG	9	11	2	2	0	4

DATE	OPPONENT	SCORE	DECISION	IP	H	R	ER	BB	K
9	@ Philadelphia	L 4-15	L (2-4)	6	12	8	6	3	0
12	@ Washington	L 4-5	L (2-5) CG	8	11	5	5	3	3
16	@ New York	L 0-3	L (2-6) CG	8	6	3	2	3	1
20	@ Boston	W 5-2	W (3-6) CG	9	9	2	1	1	3
25	@ Detroit	L 3-7	L (3-7)	4	6	4	4	0	0
27	@ Detroit	W 5-3	S (1)	3.1	1	0	0	0	1
29	Chicago	W 8-5	W (4-7) CG	9	12	5	5	2	5
June									
2	Detroit	W 9-4	W (5-7) CG	9	13	4	4	3	2
6	Washington	L 0-3	L (5-8)	8	8	2	2	0	2
10	Philadelphia	L 0-3	L (5-9)	7	6	3	3	2	4
14	Boston	W 3-0	W (6-9) SHO	9	3	0	0	1	3
18	New York	W 9-2	W (7-9) CG	9	7	2	1	3	8
22	@ Chicago	L 0-3	L (7-10)	7	6	3	3	1	3
26	St. Louis	W 6-0	W (8-10) SHO	9	6	0	0	3	6
30	@ St. Louis	L 3-10	L (8-11)	6	7	4	3	2	2
July									
4	@ Detroit	W 11-4	W (9-11) CG	9	13	4	4	2	1
8	@ New York	W 3-1	W (10-11) CG	9	8	1	1	3	3
12	@ Boston	W 11-7	W (11-11) CG	9	14	7	6	1	0
15	@ Philadelphia	W 2-0	W (12-11) SHO	9	3	0	0	4	2
19	@ Washington	W 4-1	W (13-11) CG	9	6	1	1	2	2
24	Chicago	W 5-2	W (14-11) CG	9	7	2	2	1	5
27	Philadelphia	L 2-11	L (14-12)	3.2	9	6	2	0	2
29	Washington	W 8-7		8	7	6	6	2	2
August									
2	New York	L 1-5	L (14-13)	8	9	5	2	0	5
6	Boston	W 3-2	W (15-13) CG	12	13	2	2	2	2
12	Detroit	L 5-10	L (15-14)	5	8	6	6	2	1
16	@ Philadelphia	L 9-10		6	9	7	6	2	4
19	@ Washington	W 3-1	W (16-14) CG	10	6	1	0	2	7
23	@ New York	W 4-1	W (17-14) CG	9	3	1	1	2	3

1923 Cleveland Indians

DATE	OPPONENT	SCORE	DECISION	IP	H	R	ER	BB	K
April									
18	Chicago	W 6-5		7.1	10	5	4	0	3
22	Detroit	W 1-0	W (1-0) SHO	10	5	0	0	0	1
26	@ Chicago	W 3-0	W (2-0) SHO	9	8	0	0	1	2
30	@ Detroit	W 4-2	W (3-0) CG	9	6	2	1	1	2
May									
4	St. Louis	L 5-9	L (3-1)	7	11	5	1	2	1
8	New York	L 2-3	L (3-2) CG	7	5	3	1	1	1
13	Washington	W 5-2	W (4-2) CG	9	10	2	2	2	5
16	Philadelphia	L 0-5	L (4-3)	5.2	7	3	0	0	5
20	Boston	W 1-0	W (5-3) SHO	8	6	0	0	2	2
24	@ St. Louis	W 6-1	W (6-3) CG	9	6	1	1	1	0
29	@ Chicago	W 6-4	W (7-3) CG	9	12	4	4	0	2
30	@ Chicago	W 7-6	S (1)	1.1	2	0	0	0	0

DATE	OPPONENT	SCORE	DECISION	IP	H	R	ER	BB	K
June									
2	@ Detroit	L 1-9	L (7-4)	4	9	6	5	1	0
6	@ Boston	W 17-4	W (8-4) CG	9	11	4	0	0	3
10	@ New York	L 7-8	L (8-5) CG	8.2	6	8	4	6	0
12	@ New York	W 8-4	S (2)	3	2	1	1	3	1
14	@ Philadelphia	L 3-4	L (8-6)	7	12	4	4	1	2
18	@ Washington	L 3-4	L (8-7) CG	12.1	11	4	4	2	2
23	St. Louis	L 2-8		1	2	2	0	1	0
29	Chicago	L 4-5	L (8-8)	7	10	5	4	1	1
July									
3	Detroit	L 8-12		7.2	15	8	4	0	2
7	Boston	W 27-3	W (9-8)	6	7	2	2	1	0
11	Philadelphia	W 4-2	W (10-8) CG	9	7	2	2	3	4
15	New York	L 2-4	L (10-9)	1.2	6	4	4	0	0
16	New York	W 6-0	W (11-9) SHO	9	6	0	0	1	1
19	Washington	W 3-2	W (12-9) CG	9	10	2	2	2	6
22	Washington	L 1-3	L (12-10)	8	7	3	1	1	1
25	@ St. Louis	L 2-3	L (12-11) CG	10.2	12	3	3	4	0
30	@ Boston	W 2-0	W (13-11) SHO	9	7	0	0	0	2
August									
5	@ Washington	L 5-6		3.2	5	3	3	3	0
9	@ Washington	L 1-2	L (13-12)	7.1	6	2	2	1	5
13	@ Philadelphia	L 3-14	L (13-13)	1.1	5	6	5	1	0
15	Boston	L 6-8	L (13-14)	2	8	4	4	1	0

1924 Cleveland Indians

DATE	OPPONENT	SCORE	DECISION	IP	H	R	ER	BB	K
April									
16	@ Detroit	L 1-5	L (0-1) CG	8	10	5	4	1	2
22	@ Chicago	W 7-6		8.2	15	6	6	3	1
26	@ St. Louis	L 2-11	L (0-2)	5	11	6	6	0	1
May									
2	Chicago	L 2-3	L (0-3)	8	5	3	1	1	4
7	St. Louis	L 8-10		0.2	6	6	2	1	0
11	Philadelphia	W 8-5	W (1-3) CG	9	10	5	4	4	2
17	@ Washington	L 4-6		2	2	1	1	2	0
24	@ Boston	L 2-6	L (1-4)	5.1	12	5	4	1	0
28	Chicago	L 6-13		4.2	9	6	5	1	2
June									
8	Washington	W 11-3	W (2-4) CG	9	9	3	3	2	3
12	Boston	L 3-4	L (2-5)	7	9	4	4	1	0
14	Boston	W 3-2	W (3-5)	2.1	1	0	0	0	2
16	New York	W 2-1	W (4-5) CG	9	8	1	1	5	1
20	@ Detroit	W 11-9	W (5-5)	5	5	3	1	2	1
23	@ Chicago	W 4-1	W (6-5) CG	9	4	1	1	2	1
26	@ Chicago	W 7-4	W (7-5)	2	1	0	0	0	0
28	Detroit	L 3-9	L (7-6)	5.1	5	6	5	5	2
July									
1	St. Louis	W 8-2	W (8-6) CG	9	7	2	1	1	2

DATE	OPPONENT	SCORE	DECISION	IP	H	R	ER	BB	K
4	@ Chicago	L 3-4	L (8-7)	1.1	2	1	1	0	0
6	@ Chicago	L 6-9		0.2	4	4	4	1	0
10	@ Philadelphia	W 4-3	W (9-7)	7	7	3	3	2	2
15	@ Washington	L 2-4	L (9-8) CG	8	8	4	4	4	0
19	@ New York	L 5-10	L (9-9)	7	11	9	4	4	1
23	@ Boston	L 12-16		0	3	4	4	1	0
28	Washington	W 2-1	W (10-9) CG	9	6	1	1	2	2
August									
1	Philadelphia	L 3-4	L (10-10) CG	9	9	4	2	2	3
5	Boston	W 1-0	W (11-10) SHO	9	6	0	0	3	1
9	New York	L 1-5	L (11-11) CG	9	9	5	2	2	3
13	@ Washington	W 5-1	W (12-11) CG	9	8	1	0	2	4
18	@ Philadelphia	W 13-3	W (13-11) CG	9	13	3	3	2	6
22	@ Boston	L 4-5	L (13-12) CG	8	14	5	5	2	3
27	@ New York	W 1-0	W (14-12) SHO	9	5	0	0	2	2
31	Chicago	L 1-10	L (14-13)	2.1	6	5	4	2	1
September									
3	@ St. Louis	W 9-5	W (15-13) CG	9	9	5	4	1	1
7	@ Detroit	L 7-8	L (15-14) CG	8	12	8	5	4	2
16	Washington	L 2-6	L (15-15)	8	12	6	2	1	1
22	New York	L 4-10	L (15-16) CG	9	13	10	7	3	2

1925 Washington Nationals

DATE	OPPONENT	SCORE	DECISION	IP	H	R	ER	BB	K
April									
16	@ New York	W 7-5		6	10	5	3	2	1
25	New York	W 8-7	W (1-0)	7	8	6	6	3	0
May									
2	Philadelphia	L 2-6	L (1-1)	8	7	3	3	4	6
9	@ Chicago	W 4-1	W (2-1) CG	9	5	1	1	2	1
14	@ St. Louis	W 5-3	W (3-1) CG	9	8	3	3	1	0
19	@ Cleveland	W 4-3		7	10	3	3	1	1
26	Philadelphia	W 11-2	W (4-1) CG	9	10	2	2	0	1
31	Philadelphia	W 4-3		7	6	3	2	2	4
June									
5	Chicago	W 5-3	W (5-1)	7.1	5	3	2	1	2
10	Detroit	W 11-7	W (6-1)	6	9	7	5	3	1
14	St. Louis	W 9-8		7	10	5	5	1	2
20	Cleveland	W 2-1	W (7-1) CG	9	6	1	1	2	5
25	New York	W 1-0	W (8-1) SHO	9	4	0	0	2	5
29	Philadelphia	W 4-1	W (9-1) CG	9	7	1	1	1	2
July									
3	@ Boston	W 11-0	W (10-1) SHO	9	4	0	0	5	0
8	@ Chicago	W 10-2	W (11-1) CG	9	7	2	2	1	2
12	@ St. Louis	W 5-3		5.1	7	3	3	3	2
16	@ Detroit	W 2-1	W (12-1) CG	10	6	1	0	6	2
20	@ Cleveland	W 9-1	W (13-1) CG	9	8	1	1	1	3
26	@ New York	W 7-4	W (14-1)	8	6	4	4	4	0
30	Chicago	L 1-11	L (14-2)	3	9	5	5	0	0

DATE	OPPONENT	SCORE	DECISION	IP	H	R	ER	BB	K
August									
3	Detroit	L 2-3	L (14-3)	5	5	3	3	3	1
7	St. Louis	L 0-3	L (14-4)	5	4	3	3	1	3
11	Cleveland	W 3-1	W (15-4) CG	9	11	1	1	1	1
15	New York	W 6-1	W (16-4) CG	9	8	1	1	4	1
21	@ Detroit	L 0-1	L (16-5)	10	11	1	1	2	1
26	@ St. Louis	L 8-11		2	4	3	3	2	0
September									
2	Philadelphia	W 8-5	W (17-5)	8	11	5	5	2	2
7	@ Philadelphia	W 7-6		6.1	8	5	5	4	0
12	Boston	W 13-3	W (18-5) CG	9	6	3	2	3	2
17	Detroit	W 1-0	W (19-5) SHO	6	5	0	0	3	3
22	Cleveland	W 3-2	W (20-5) CG	9	6	2	2	2	2

1926 Washington Nationals

DATE	OPPONENT	SCORE	DECISION	IP	H	R	ER	BB	K
April									
14	Philadelphia	W 3-1	W (1-0) CG	9	6	1	0	1	2
21	@ Philadelphia	L 2-5	L (1-1)	7	10	4	0	4	1
25	Boston	L 6-8		7.1	10	3	3	1	2
30	@ New York	L 2-7	L (1-2)	7	10	7	7	4	0
May									
5	@ Boston	W 11-0	W (2-2) SHO	9	4	0	0	4	1
10	Chicago	L 0-2	L (2-3)	8	6	2	2	3	2
15	Cleveland	W 6-4	W (3-3) CG	9	7	4	3	2	1
20	Detroit	L 5-6		5	10	5	5	2	0
25	@ Philadelphia	W 17-12		3	5	4	3	2	1
29	Boston	W 4-2	W (4-3)	8.1	11	2	1	3	1
June									
5	@ Detroit	W 8-4	W (5-3) CG	9	8	4	4	1	1
10	@ Cleveland	W 5-3	W (6-3)	8	8	3	3	2	4
15	@ Chicago	L 1-4	L (6-4)	7	6	4	1	3	3
19	@ St. Louis	L 4-9	L (6-5)	3	6	5	1	3	0
24	@ Philadelphia	W 8-6		5	7	4	4	1	3
29	@ Boston	L 1-2	L (6-6)	7	6	2	1	1	3
July									
4	New York	T 4-4	CG	6	6	4	2	2	3
10	St. Louis	W 19-4	W (7-6)	5	8	3	2	1	1
14	Chicago	L 2-10	L (7-7)	4	7	6	2	3	1
18	Cleveland	L 3-5	L (7-8) CG	9	7	5	4	5	0
23	Detroit	L 6-9	L (7-9)	5	11	5	5	3	2
25	Detroit	L 4-14		2	3	1	1	2	0
30	@ Chicago	L 4-5		7.2	10	3	3	0	4
August									
4	@ Detroit	L 4-5		7	9	4	4	1	0
7	@ Cleveland	W 9-2	W (8-9) CG	9	10	2	2	3	3
11	New York	W 5-4		5	8	4	2	2	1
15	Philadelphia	W 5-3	W (9-9)	8	8	3	1	3	0
22	Cleveland	L 0-6	L (9-10)	8	14	6	5	2	2

DATE	OPPONENT	SCORE	DECISION	IP	H	R	ER	BB	K
26	Chicago	W 1-0	W (10-10) SHO	10	4	0	0	4	0
31	@ Boston	W 2-0	W (11-10) SHO	9	5	0	0	2	0
September									
1	@ Boston	W 14-12		1.1	0	0	0	1	0
5	Boston	W 6-2	W (12-10) CG	9	8	2	2	1	2
11	@ Cleveland	L 2-3	L (12-11)	7.1	9	3	2	2	3
16	@ Detroit	W 3-2	W (13-11)	6.1	10	1	1	3	2
20	@ St. Louis	W 7-4	W (14-11) CG	9	9	4	4	4	0
25	@ Chicago	W 3-2		6	6	2	2	4	1

1927 Washington Nationals

DATE	OPPONENT	SCORE	DECISION	IP	H	R	ER	BB	K
April									
12	Boston	W 6-2	W (1-0)	4	4	1	1	1	0
22	@ Boston	W 7-3	W (2-0)	6	2	1	1	3	1
May									
2	New York	L 6-9	L (2-1)	2	5	4	2	0	1
3	New York	L 4-6		0.1	1	0	0	2	1
8	@ St. Louis	L 3-8		2	1	1	1	2	0

1928 New York Yankees

DATE	OPPONENT	SCORE	DECISION	IP	H	R	ER	BB	K
May									
2	@ Washington	L 5-9		2	0	0	0	1	0
6	Chicago	W 4-2	W (1-0)	6.1	7	2	2	2	2
12	Detroit	W 8-7		2	6	5	5	1	0
17	St. Louis	W 4-3	W (2-0) CG	9	6	3	2	1	0
22	Boston	W 14-4	W (3-0) CG	9	8	4	4	2	1
26	@ Philadelphia	W 7-4	W (4-0)	5.2	8	4	4	1	0
June									
10	@ Chicago	L 6-8		6.1	5	5	5	6	0
30	@ Boston	W 7-6	W (5-0)	7	9	4	4	2	0
July									
9	St. Louis	L 6-12	L (5-1)	1.1	7	5	5	0	1
23	@ Boston	L 3-8		2	1	0	0	0	0
28	@ Cleveland	L 4-9		5.1	11	5	5	2	1
August									
3	@ St. Louis	L 0-8		1.2	4	4	1	2	0

Information was obtained free of charge from and is copyrighted by Retrosheet. Interested parties may contact Retrosheet at "www.retrosheet.org".

Additional statistics compiled from:

Baseball-reference.com, Sports Reference LLC

Baseball-almanac.com

The Plain Dealer, Cleveland, archives

Tom Kutza at the Stan Coveleski memorial during a Shamokin history tour on November 28, 2020. (Photo courtesy of *The News-Item*, Shamokin.)

Advertisement for liniment featuring Stan Coveleski that was published in the *Shamokin News-Dispatch* on March 1, 1927.

Rosalie Coveleski Moyer, front, with her brother John Jr., great uncle Stan, and father John in July 1969. (Photo courtesy of Rosalie Coveleski Moyer.)

Stan Coveleski, fourth from left, in 1969 with sons of his brother Frank. From left, Harry, Jack, Joe, Stan, Bill, Pepi (Robert), and Stanley. Frank named several of his sons after his brothers. (Photo courtesy of grandchildren of Frank Coveleskie.)

Afterword

Stan Coveleski's life is an interesting story, but it literally hit home for me because of the connection to our shared hometown of Shamokin and the coal mines. Although I didn't experience work in the mines, members of my family did, including my grandfather, who was injured in an accident at the Cameron Colliery in 1930 and could not do physical work again.

I never had the opportunity to meet Covey. I wish I had. By writing this book, I've gotten to know a little about the man, the challenges he faced, and the success he enjoyed. He is someone I won't forget, and I hope through this book, others will learn about and remember the man who escaped the coal mines by throwing rocks at tin cans and became a Hall of Fame baseball pitcher. A man they called the Silent Pole. A man known as Covey.

Endnotes

Chapter 1
1. Steve Steinberg telephone interview, October 30, 2021.
2. Department of the Interior, Bureau of Mines report, "Coal-mine fatalities in the United States 1870–1914," p. 281.
3. Ibid., p. 286.
4. Www.phmc.pa.gov/Archives/Research-Online/Pages/Molly-Maguires.
5. Department of the Interior, Bureau of Mines report, "Coal-mine fatalities in the United States 1870–1914," p. 285.
6. Pennsylvania Historical & Museum Commission, Manuscript Group 463, Susquehanna Coal Company records, 1878–1916.

Chapter 2
1. Britannica.com/story/who-really-invented-baseball by Tim Newcomb.
2. ESPN: espn.com/blog/sportscenter/post/_/id/60572/this-day-in-sports-the-first-official-baseball -game-officially-happens.
3. Harry Coveleski bio by John Heiselman for the Society for American Baseball Research. sabr.org /bioproj/person/harry-coveleski.
4. Tom Kutza radio interview, June 30, 1969.
5. Ibid.
6. Statscrew.com.
7. Jake Daubert bio by Jim Sandoval for the Society for American Baseball Research.
8. Baseball-almanac.com.
9. Ibid.

Chapter 3
1. Tom Kutza radio interview, June 30, 1969.
2. Rod Roberts audio interview for the Hall of Fame, August 22, 1981.
3. Baseball-reference.com.
4. *The Philadelphia Inquirer,* September 13, 1912, p. 10.
5. Based on an unsourced transcript of an interview with Coveleski that the Hall of Fame has on file.
6. Joe McGinnity bio by Don Doxsie for Society for American Baseball Research: sabr.org/bioproj /person/joe-mcginnity.
7. Based on an unsourced transcript of an interview with Coveleski that the Hall of Fame has on file.
8. Baseball Reference: baseball-reference.com/bullpen/Deadball_Era.
9. *The Columbus Dispatch,* Columbus, Ohio, January 23, 1905, p. 11.
10. *The Denver Post,* Colorado, January 3, 1905, p. 13.

Chapter 4
1. MLB Timeline: mlb.com/guardians/history/timeline.
2. Baseball-reference.com.
3. Southsidesox.com, Jim Margalus, Aug. 20, 2015.
4. Baseball-reference.com.
5. Scott Longert, "The Best They Could Be: How the Cleveland Indians Became the Kings of Baseball, 1916-1920," p. 20.
6. *The Plain Dealer,* Cleveland, January 9, 1922, p. 15.

7. Ballparksofbaseball.com.
8. *The Plain Dealer*, Cleveland, April 18, 1916, p. 11.
9. Ibid., May 31, 1916, p. 13.
10. Mlb.com/cut4/this-day-in-baseball-history-the-yankees-become-the-first-mlb-team-to-put-number.
11. Scott Longert, "The Best They Could Be: How the Cleveland Indians Became the Kings of Baseball, 1916–1920," p. 62.
12. Eugene Murdock audio interview, May 13, 1974, on file at Cleveland Public Library.
13. Centers for Disease Control and Prevention: cdc.gov/flu/pandemic-resources/1918-commemoration/1918-pandemic-history.
14. Scott Longert, "The Best They Could Be: How the Cleveland Indians Became the Kings of Baseball, 1916–1920," p. 88.
15. *The Plain Dealer*, Cleveland, May 25, 1918, p. 13.
16. Scott Longert, "The Best They Could Be: How the Cleveland Indians Became the Kings of Baseball, 1916–1920," p. 99.
17. Baseballhall.org/discover-more/stories/short-stops/1918-world-war-i-baseball.
18. Mlb.com/news/babe-ruth-715th-home-run.
19. Worldseries.com: World Series History.
20. Mike Huber for Society for American Baseball research: "September 5, 1918: Babe Ruth tosses shutout in Game 1 as patriotism prevails in World Series opener": sabr.org/gamesproj/game/september-5-1918-babe-ruth-tosses-shutout-as-patriotism-prevails-in-opening-of-fall-classic.
21. *The Plain Dealer*, Cleveland, July 20, 1919, p. 1C.
22. Scott Longert, "The Best They Could Be: How the Cleveland Indians Became the Kings of Baseball, 1916–1920," p. 135.
23. *The Plain Dealer*, Cleveland, Monday, Aug. 25, 1919, page 10; Scott Longert, "The Best They Could Be: How Cleveland Indians Became the Kings of Baseball, 1916-1920" Page 138; "The incredible story of Ray Caldwell, the MLB pitcher who survived a lightning strike to finish a game," by Ryan Hockensmith: espn.com/mlb/story/_/id/32061845/the-incredible-story-mlb-pitcher-survived-lightning-strike-finish-game.

Chapter 5

1. Baseball historian and author Steve Steinberg article "The Spitball and the End of the Deadball Era" for the Society for American Baseball Research's "The National Pastime" Vol. 23 in 2003.
2. Eugene Murdock audio interview, May 13, 1974, on file at Cleveland Public Library.
3. *The Plain Dealer*, Cleveland, November 5, 1919, p. 18.
4. Steve Steinberg, telephone interview October 23, 2021.
5. From baseball historian and author Steve Steinberg's article "The Spitball and the End of the Deadball Era" for the Society for American Baseball Research's "The National Pastime" Vol. 23 in 2003: sabr.org/research/article/the-spitball-and-the-end-of-the-deadball-era.
6. *The Plain Dealer*, Cleveland, February 29, 1920, p. 21.
7. Some details from Cleveland.com.
8. *The Plain Dealer*, Cleveland, May 29, 1920, p. 16.
9. Ibid., July 15, p. 18.
10. Story about Chapman's death based on numerous sources, including 1920 stories from *The Plain Dealer*, Cleveland; "The most tragic pitch in MLB history, 100 years later" by Mike Vaccaro, August 15, 2020, nypost.com/2020/08/15/100-years-ago-a-yankees-pitch-killed-ray-chapman/amp; pitcherlist.com/this-week-in-baseball-history-aug-16-22.
11. *The Plain Dealer*, Cleveland, "Ban Johnson Will Take No Action Against Carl Mays For His Pitching," August 21, 1920, p. 12.
12. Eugene Murdock audio interview, May 13, 1974, on file at Cleveland Public Library.
13. *The Plain Dealer*, Cleveland, October 26, 1922, p. 18.

Chapter 6

1. *Washington Herald*, Washington, D.C., October 6, 1920, p. 9.
2. *The Plain Dealer*, Cleveland, "Tribe's Hurlers Equal Dodgers', Speaker says," October 6, 1920, p. 16.

Endnotes

3. Ibid., "Speaker Gives Grimes Credit for Box Work," October 7, 1920, p. 20.
4. Ibid., October 8, 1920, p. 1.
5. Society for American Baseball Research: "October 9, 1920: Coveleski stops Brooklyn to tie World Series at 2-2," by Joseph Wancho: sabr.org/gamesproj/game/october-9-1920-coveleski-stops-brooklyn -to-tie-world-series-at-2-2.
6. *The Plain Dealer*, Cleveland, October 9, 1920, p. 1.
7. Ibid., p. 14.
8. Ibid., October 10, 1920, p. 1B.
9. Ibid., p. 1B.
10. Ibid., p. 2B.
11. Eugene Murdock audio interview, May 13, 1974, on file at Cleveland Public Library.
12. Details from Society for American Baseball Research article "October 10, 1920: A game of World Series firsts: unassisted triple play and grand slam" by Joseph Wancho.
13. *The Plain Dealer*, Cleveland, "Proud of Every Indian in Game Spoke Declares," October 11, 1920, p. 15.
14. Ibid., "Mails Defeats Smith 1-0 in Pitching Duel," October 12, 1920, p. 1.
15. Ibid., "Speaker Hands George Burns Pretty Bouquet," October 12, 1920, p. 17.
16. Ibid., "Pitcher in Doubt for Game Today," October 12, 1920, p. 1.
17. Ibid., "Robins Sure of Victory Today," October 12, 1920, p. 18.
18. Scott Longert, "The Best They Could Be: How the Cleveland Indians Became the Kings of Baseball, 1916–1920," p. 236.
19. *The Plain Dealer*, Cleveland, October 13, 1920, p. 19.
20. Ibid., p. 18.
21. Ibid., p. 18.
22. Ibid., p. 21.
23. Ibid., "Covey's Pitching Is Best of Any Hurler in Series," October 13, 1920, p. 18.
24. Stan Coveleski profile, National Baseball Hall of Fame: baseballhall.org/hall-of-famers/coveleski-stan.
25. *The Plain Dealer*, Cleveland, October 14, 1920, p. 18.
26. Ibid., "Raise purse for Covey," October 17, 1920, p. 24.

Chapter 7

1. *The Plain Dealer*, Cleveland, March 6, 1921, p. 19.
2. Ibid., February 27, 1921, p. 19.
3. Ibid., December 23, 1921, p. 16.
4. Society for American Baseball Research profile by Charles F. Faber: sabr.org/bioproj/person/allen -sothoron.
5. Society for American Baseball Research, "Allen Sothoron" by Charles F. Faber: sabr.org/bioproj /person/allen-sothoron.
6. *The Plain Dealer*, Cleveland, May 17, 1921, p. 20.
7. Ibid., September 3, 1921, p. 14.
8. Ibid., March 9, 1922, p. 16.
9. Ibid., July 16, 1922, p. 33.
10. Ibid., August 31, 1922, p. 18.
11. Ibid., September 16, 1922, p. 15.
12. Society for American Baseball Research, "Cleveland Indians team ownership history" by David Bohmer: sabr.org/bioproj/topic/cleveland-indians-team-ownership-history.
13. This Day in Baseball by The Associated Press.
14. *The Plain Dealer*, Cleveland, August 16, 1923, p. 26.
15. Ibid., August 25, 1923, p. 14.
16. Ibid., August 29, 1923, p. 17.
17. *Shamokin News-Dispatch*, February 1, 1924, p. 1.
18. *The Plain Dealer*, Cleveland, February 14, 1924, p. 16.
19. Ibid., March 12, 1924, p. 20.
20. Ibid., February 19, 1924, p. 16.

21. Ibid., April 6, 1924, p. 51.
22. Ibid., December 12, 1924, p. 22.
23. Eugene Murdock audio interview, May 13, 1974, on file at Cleveland Public Library.
24. Society for American Baseball Research, "Stan Coveleski" bio by Daniel R. Levitt: sabr.org/bioproj
    /person/stan-coveleski.
25. *The Plain Dealer,* Cleveland, December 14, 1924, p. 34.
26. *Evening Star,* Washington, D.C., February 12, 1925, p. 30.
27. *The Plain Dealer,* Cleveland, March 8, 1925, p. 18.
28. *Shamokin News-Dispatch,* "My Shamokin" by Edgar Marlock, May 12, 1956, p. 4.
29. *The Plain Dealer,* Cleveland, September 25, 1925, p. 18.
30. *Evening Star,* Washington, D.C., October 1, 1925, p. 28.
31. Ibid., September 21, 1925, p. 25.
32. *The Plain Dealer,* Cleveland, October 8, 1925, p. 7.
33. Ibid., October 9, 1925, p. 20.
34. *Evening Star,* Washington, D.C., October 12, 1925, p. 26.
35. Ibid., October 13, 1925, p. 27.
36. *The Plain Dealer,* Cleveland October 17, 1925, p. 16.
37. *Evening Star,* Washington, D.C., October 15, 1925, p. 28.
38. Ibid., February 19, 1926, p. 38.
39. Ibid., March 9, 1927, p. 31.
40. Ibid., February 18, 1927, p. 39
41. Ibid., March 15, 1927, p. 52.
42. Ibid., April 6, 1927, p. 31.
43. Ibid., May 10, 1927, p. 29.
44. Ibid., May 29, 1927, p. 42.
45. Ibid., June 2, 1927, p. 36.
46. *Shamokin News-Dispatch,* July 9, 1927, p. 6.
47. *The Plain Dealer,* Cleveland, June 19, 1927, p. 16.
48. Ibid., July 12, 1927, p. 19.
49. *Shamokin News-Dispatch,* July 9, 1927, p. 6.
50. United Press, The Cincinnati Post, December 22, 1927, p. 14.
51. Shamokin News-Dispatch, January 31, 1928.
52. *Evening Star,* Washington, D.C., October 3, 1928, p. 34.

Chapter 8

1. *Shamokin News-Dispatch,* March 19, 1929, p. 1.
2. Rod Roberts audio interview for the Hall of Fame, August 22, 1981.
3. Ibid.
4. NEA Service, *The Indianapolis Times,* April 1, 1931, p. 13.
5. *Shamokin News-Dispatch,* July 20, 1938, p. 2.
6. *The Plain Dealer,* Cleveland, July 4, 1938, p. 18.
7. Rod Roberts audio interview for the Hall of Fame, August 22, 1981.
8. The Associated Press, March 28, 1945.
9. *Shamokin News-Dispatch,* August 26, 1964, p. 13.
10. Rod Roberts audio interview for the Hall of Fame, August 22, 1981.
11. United Press International, February 3, 1969.
12. *Reading Eagle,* July 6, 1969, p. 54.
13. "Induction Day at Cooperstown: A History of the Baseball Hall of Fame Ceremony" by Dennis
    Corcoran, McFarland & Company, 2010.
14. Rod Roberts audio interview for the Hall of Fame, August 22, 1981.
15. "Waite Hoyt: A Biography of the Yankees' Schoolboy Wonder" by William A. Cook, p. 188,
    McFarland, 2004.
16. The Associated Press, July 31, 1969.
17. *Rockford Morning Star,* Illinois, June 26, 1977, p. 57.

18. Rod Roberts audio interview for the Hall of Fame, August 22, 1981.
19. Ibid.
20. The Associated Press, *The Plain Dealer*, Cleveland, March 21, 1984, p. 65.
21. *South Bend Tribune*, March 21, 1984, page 17.
22. Tom Kutza telephone interview November 1, 2021.

Chapter 9

1. Tom Kutza telephone interview November 1, 2021.
2. *The Plain Dealer*, Cleveland, February 23, 1921, p. 14.
3. Ibid., June 19, 1921, p. 3B.
4. Society for American Baseball Research biography project, Stan Coveleski: sabr.org/bioproj/person/stan-coveleski.
5. Rod Roberts audio interview for the Hall of Fame, August 22, 1981.
6. *Chicago Daily News*, January 15, 1953, p. 34.
7. Rod Roberts audio interview for the Hall of Fame, 1986.
8. *The Plain Dealer*, Cleveland, October 10, 1920, p. 1B.
9. *Houston Chronicle*, July 6, 1937, p. 20.
10. United Press International, *Evening Star*, Washington, D.C., February 3, 1969, p. 16.
11. *Chicago Daily News*, July 17, 1970, John P. Carmichael column, p. 6.
12. Tom Kutza radio interview, June 30, 1969.
13. *The Plain Dealer*, Cleveland, May 29, 1975, p. 74.
14. *Shamokin News-Dispatch*, 1927, p. 6.
15. Baseball-Reference.com via Michael Haupert research of Hall of Fame contracts.
16. United Press International, *Evening Star*, Washington, D.C., February 3, 1969, p. 16.
17. Telephone interview, October 23, 2021.
18. Ibid., November 4, 2021.
19. Ibid., November 1, 2021.
20. Ibid., January 11, 2022.
21. Ibid., 2021.
22. Ibid., 2021.
23. Ibid., January 18, 2022.

Sources

Society for American Baseball Research.

Recorded radio interview by Tom Kutza, June 30, 1969, for WISL-AM, Shamokin, Pennsylvania.

Society for American Baseball Research, "Stan Coveleski" bio by Daniel R. Levitt: sabr.org/bioproj/person/stan-coveleski.

National Baseball Hall of Fame and Museum, including an unsourced transcription of an audio interview with Coveleski.

Stan Coveleski oral history interview, 1981 August 23, CTA 792, Rod Roberts Oral History collection, BA RMA 001, National Baseball Hall of Fame and Museum.

"The Best They Could Be: How the Cleveland Indians Became the Kings of Baseball, 1916–1920," by Scott H. Longert. Potomac Books, 2013.

"The Glory of Their Times: The Story of the Early Days of Baseball Told by the Men Who Played It," by Lawrence S. Ritter (1922–2004). Harper Perennial Modern Classics, 2010.

Alek Washuta documentary, "Covey: The story of Stan Coveleski," May 3, 1921. (youtube.com/watch?v=d2kylrD-KTM)

Recorded audio interview by Eugene Murdock (1921–1992), May 13, 1984, on file at the Cleveland Public Library. (Murdock's interview with Coveleski is part of the Cleveland Public Library Digital Gallery.)

Retrosheet, Baseball Reference (baseball-reference.com) and Baseball Almanac (baseball-almanac.com), which have team records and player statistics, including information from the early days of baseball. In some cases, those early details don't match, probably because they were taken from handwritten paper files. Most stats used in this book were from Baseball Reference.

Numerous newspaper archives, including *The Plain Dealer,* Cleveland; the *Evening Star,* Washington, D.C.; the *Shamokin News-Dispatch,* Shamokin, Pennsylvania; and others listed in the endnotes

Cleveland Public Library

Detroit Public Library

The History Museum, South Bend, Indiana

Acknowledgments

Bruce Victoriano and his father Ralph

Tom Kutza, WISL radio announcer

Scott Longert, baseball author and historian, for his support and encouragement

Steve Steinberg, baseball author and historian, for his advice and for sharing numerous photos from his private collection

Cassidy Lent and Roger Lansing, National Baseball Hall of Fame

Jeremy Feader, Cleveland Guardians historian

Dr. Ann Yezerski

Larry Deklinski

Jarad Zarkowski

Sarah Dobransky, Cleveland Public Library

Carla Reczek, Librarian III Specialist, Detroit Public Library

Travis Childs, The History Museum, South Bend, Indiana

Stan Coveleski family members

Special thanks to Rosalie Coveleski Moyer, Stan's great-great niece, who shared memories and helped me to connect with other family members.

Thanks to the following nieces and nephews, who shared their memories and family stories about Covey:

John E. Coveleski

Frank Kibler

Kathy and Bob Lavelle

Larry Cove

Bill Covaleskie

Patricia Heisse

About the Author

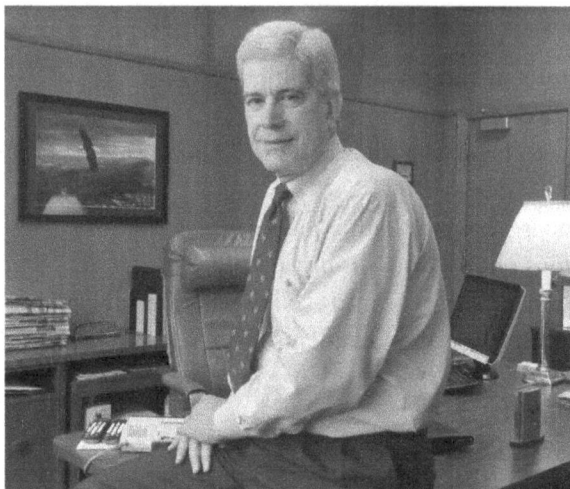

Harry J. Deitz Jr. worked in the newspaper business for 45 years as a photographer, sportswriter, sports editor, design editor, and editor. He retired in 2018 after 10 years as editor-in-chief of the Reading Eagle, Reading, Pa.

In his weekly "Editor's Notebook" column, he wrote extensively about his family—parents, grandparents, three children and especially six grandchildren—and shared his personal story of his six years as the primary caregiver for his late wife during her battle with Parkinson's disease and cancer.

He has served as president and board member of the Pennsylvania Newsmedia Association and the Pennsylvania Associated Press Managing Editors and has won numerous awards for his columns, sportswriting and newspaper design work.

In his spare time, he has hiked the entire Pennsylvania section of the Appalachian Trail and has read every book by novelist Ken Follett.

Harry is a native of Shamokin, Pa., where he followed his father into newspaper work. He is the author of "Our Father's Journey: A Path Out of Poverty" and "Journal of a Caregiver: A Story of Love and Devotion."

www.ingramcontent.com/pod-product-compliance
Lightning Source LLC
Chambersburg PA
CBHW011201090426
42742CB00020B/3410